LECTURES
ON FAITH

Cover painting, *Go with Me to Cumorah* © Liz Lemon Swindle, Repartee & Foundation Arts

Published by Covenant Communications, Inc.
American Fork, Utah

Printed in Canada
First Printing: March 2000

10 09 08 07 06 05   14 13 12 11 10 9 8

ISBN 1-57734-637-8

LECTURES
ON FAITH

DELIVERED DURING 1834 AND 1835 TO
THE SCHOOL OF THE ELDERS IN KIRTLAND, OHIO

First Published by the Church of Jesus Christ of Latter-day Saints

Covenant Communications, Inc.

Covenant

CONTENTS

PREFACE TO THIS EDITION

These seven lectures were originally prepared in connection with the school of the elders in Kirtland, Ohio, and were subsequently published as part of the 1835 Doctrine and Covenants. They were maintained as an integral portion of that book until the 1921 edition, when they were removed on the basis that "they were never presented to nor accepted by the church as being otherwise than theological lectures or lessons."

While never having been approved by the church as a canonical element of scripture, their value has been praised by many and they continue to hold a position of unique interest among Latter-day Saint scholars. Many of the ideas presented in these lectures offer wonderful insights into the restored doctrines of the gospel and the centrality of the role of Christ as the Savior of mankind.

Over the years, an ongoing scholarly debate has attempted to discern the lectures' author. Many have desired to attribute the writing to Joseph Smith, either directly or under his careful approval. But while it is clear that the Prophet gave his consent to the 1835 publication, it is a far more complicated matter to determine his level of involvement in or acceptance of the lectures themselves. There is strong evidence to indicate that at least the majority of the writing was undertaken by Sidney Rigdon, who was then a member of the First Presidency. His voice and philosophical approach to logical exposition resonate throughout the lectures, providing the modern reader with a fascinating firsthand view of what it may have been like to attend the school of the elders and receive instruction under the powerful tutelage of the early leaders of the Church.

In this edition, we have made minor changes in spelling and punctuation and have included the scriptural citations within the text for easier reference.

LECTURE FIRST

1. Faith being the first principle in revealed religion, and the foundation of all righteousness, necessarily claims the first place in a course of lectures which are designed to unfold to the understanding the doctrine of Jesus Christ.

2. In presenting the subject of faith, we shall observe the following order:

3. First, faith itself—what it is.

4. Secondly, the object on which it rests. And,

5. Thirdly, the effects which flow from it.

6. Agreeable to this order we have first to show what faith is.

7. The author of the epistle to the Hebrews, in the eleventh chapter of that epistle and first verse, gives the following definition of the word faith:

8. "Now faith is the substance (assurance) of things hoped for, the evidence of things not seen."

9. From this we learn that faith is the assurance which men have of the existence of things which they have not seen, and the principle of action in all intelligent beings.

10. If men were duly to consider themselves, and turn their thoughts and reflections to the operations of their own minds, they would readily discover that it is faith, and faith only, which is the moving cause of all action in them; that without it both mind and body would be in a state of inactivity, and all their exertions would cease, both physical and mental.

11. Were this class to go back and reflect upon the history of their lives, from the period of their first recollection, and ask themselves what principle excited them to action, or what gave

them energy and activity in all their lawful avocations, callings, and pursuits, what would be the answer? Would it not be that it was the assurance which they had of the existence of things which they had not seen as yet? Was it not the hope which you had, in consequence of your belief in the existence of unseen things, which stimulated you to action and exertion in order to obtain them? Are you not dependent on your faith, or belief, for the acquisition of all knowledge, wisdom, and intelligence? Would you exert yourselves to obtain wisdom and intelligence, unless you did believe that you could obtain them? Would you have ever sown, if you had not believed that you would reap? Would you have ever planted, if you had not believed that you would gather? Would you have ever asked, unless you had believed that you would receive? Would you have ever sought unless you had believed that you would have found? Or, would you have ever knocked, unless you had believed that it would have been opened unto you? In a word, is there anything that you would have done, either physical or mental, if you had not previously believed? Are not all your exertions of every kind, dependent on your faith? Or, may we not ask, what have you, or what do you possess, which you have not obtained by reason of your faith? Your food, your raiment, your lodgings—are they not all by reason of your faith? Reflect, and ask yourselves if these things are not so. Turn your thoughts on your own minds, and see if faith is not the moving cause of all action in yourselves; and, if the moving cause in you, is it not in all other intelligent beings?

12. And as faith is the moving cause of all action in temporal concerns, so it is in spiritual; for the Saviour has said, and that truly, that "He that believeth and is baptized shall be saved," (Mark 16:16).

13. As we receive by faith all temporal blessings that we do receive, so we in like manner receive by faith all spiritual blessings that we do receive. But faith is not only the principle of action, but of power also, in all intelligent beings, whether in heaven or on earth. Thus says the author of the epistle to the Hebrews (11:3):

14. "Through faith we understand that the worlds were framed by the word of God, so that things which are seen were not made of things which do appear."

15. By this we understand that the principle of power which existed in the bosom of God, by which the worlds were framed, was faith; and that it is by reason of this principle of power existing in the Deity, that all created things exist; so that all things in heaven, on earth, or under the earth, exist by reason of faith as it existed in Him.

16. Had it not been for the principle of faith the worlds would never have been framed, neither would man have been formed of the dust. It is the principle by which Jehovah works, and through which he exercises power over all temporal as well as eternal things. Take this principle or attribute—for it is an attribute—from the Deity, and he would cease to exist.

17. Who cannot see, that if God framed the worlds by faith, that it is by faith that he exercises power over them, and that faith is the principle of power? And if the principle of power, it must be so in man as well as in the Deity? This is the testimony of all the sacred writers and the lesson which they have been endeavoring to teach to man.

18. The Saviour says (Matthew 17:19-20), in explaining the reason why the disciples could not cast out the devil, that it was because of their unbelief: "For verily I say unto you," said he, "if ye have faith as a grain of mustard seed, ye shall say unto this mountain, Remove hence to yonder place, and it shall remove; and nothing shall be impossible unto you."

19. Moroni, while abridging and compiling the record of his fathers, has given us the following account of faith as the principle of power. He says (Ether 12:13) that it was the faith of Alma and Amulek which caused the walls of the prison to be rent, as recorded (Alma 14:23-29); it was the faith of Nephi and Lehi which caused a change to be wrought upon the hearts of the Lamanites, when they were immersed with the Holy Spirit and with fire, as seen (Helaman 5:37-50); and that it was by faith the mountain Zerin was removed when the

brother of Jared spake in the name of the Lord. (See also Ether 12:30.)

20. In addition to this we are told in Hebrews 11:32–35, that Gideon, Barak, Samson, Jephthah, David, Samuel, and the prophets, through faith subdued kingdoms, wrought righteousness, obtained promises, stopped the mouths of lions, quenched the violence of fire, escaped the edge of the sword; out of weakness were made strong, waxed valiant in fight, turned to flight the armies of the aliens, and that women received their dead raised to life again, etc.

21. Also Joshua, in the sight of all Israel, bade the sun and moon to stand still, and it was done (Joshua 10:12–13).

22. We here understand, that the sacred writers say that all these things were done by faith. It was by faith that the worlds were framed. God spake, chaos heard, and worlds came into order by reason of the faith there was in Him. So with man also; he spake by faith in the name of God, and the sun stood still, the moon obeyed, mountains removed, prisons fell, lions' mouths were closed, the human heart lost its enmity, fire its violence, armies their power, the sword its terror, and death its dominion; and all this by reason of the faith which was in him.

23. Had it not been for the faith which was in men, they might have spoken to the sun, the moon, the mountains, prisons, the human heart, fire, armies, the sword, or to death in vain!

24. Faith, then, is the first great governing principle which has power, dominion, and authority over all things; by it they exist, by it they are upheld, by it they are changed, or by it they remain, agreeable to the will of God. Without it there is no power, and without power there could be no creation nor existence!

QUESTIONS AND ANSWERS ON THE FOREGOING PRINCIPLES

25. What is theology?

It is that revealed science which treats of the being and attributes of God, his relations to us, the dispensations of his providence, his will with respect to our actions, and his purposes with respect to our end (*Buck's Theological Dictionary*, page 582).

26. What is the first principle in this revealed science?
Faith (Lecture 1:1).

27. Why is faith the first principle in this revealed science?
Because it is the foundation of all righteousness. Hebrews 11:6: "Without faith it is impossible to please [God]." 1 John 3:7: "Little children, let no man deceive you: he that doeth righteousness is righteous, even as he [God] is righteous," (Lecture 1:1).

28. What arrangement should be followed in presenting the subject of faith?
First, it should be shown what faith is (Lecture 1:3). Secondly, the object upon which it rests (Lecture 1:4). And, thirdly, the effects which flow from it (Lecture 1:5).

29. What is faith?
It is the assurance of things hoped for, the evidence of things not seen (Hebrews 11:1); that is, it is the assurance we have of the existence of unseen things. And being the assurance which we have of the existence of unseen things, must be the principle of action in all intelligent beings. Hebrews 11:3: "Through faith we understand that the worlds were framed by the word of God," (Lecture 1:8-9).

30. How do you prove that faith is the principle of action in all intelligent beings?
First, by duly considering the operations of my own mind; and, secondly, by the direct declaration of scripture. Hebrews 11:7: "By faith Noah, being warned of God of things not seen as yet, moved with fear, prepared an ark to the saving of his house; by the which he condemned the world, and became heir

of the righteousness which is by faith." Hebrews 11:8: "By faith Abraham, when he was called to go out into a place which he should after receive for an inheritance, obeyed; and he went out, not knowing whither he went." Hebrews 11:9: "By faith he sojourned in the land of promise, as in a strange country, dwelling in tabernacles with Isaac and Jacob, the heirs with him of the same promise." Hebrews 11:27: By faith Moses "forsook Egypt, not fearing the wrath of the king: for he endured, as seeing him who is invisible," (Lecture 1:10–11).

31. Is not faith the principle of action in spiritual things as well as in temporal?
    It is.

32. How do you prove it?
    Hebrews 11:6: "Without faith it is impossible to please [God]." Mark 16:16: "He that believeth and is baptized shall be saved." Romans 4:16: "Therefore it is of faith, that it might be by grace; to the end the promise might be sure to all the seed; not to that only which is of the law, but to that also which is of the faith of Abraham; who is the father of us all," (Lecture 1:12–13).

33. Is faith anything else beside the principle of action?
    It is.

34. What is it?
    It is the principle of power also (Lecture 1:13).

35. How do you prove it?
    First, it is the principle of power in the Deity as well as in man. Hebrews 11:3: "Through faith we understand that the worlds were framed by the word of God, so that things which are seen were not made of things which do appear," (Lecture 1:14–16). Secondly, it is the principle of power in man also. Book of Mormon (Alma 14:23-29):

Alma and Amulek are delivered from prison. Helaman 5:37–50: Nephi and Lehi, with the Lamanites, are immersed with the Spirit. Ether 12:30: The mountain Zerin, by the faith of the brother of Jared, is removed. Joshua 10:12: "Then spake Joshua to the Lord in the day when the Lord delivered up the Amorites before the children of Israel, and he said in the sight of Israel, Sun, stand thou still upon Gibeon; and thou, Moon, in the valley of Ajalon." Joshua 10:13: "And the sun stood still, and the moon stayed, until the people had avenged themselves upon their enemies. Is not this written in the book of Jasher? So the sun stood still in the midst of heaven, and hasted not to go down about a whole day." Matthew 17:19: "Then came the disciples to Jesus apart, and said, Why could not we cast him out?" Matthew 17:20: "And Jesus said unto them, Because of your unbelief; for verily I say unto you, if ye have faith as a grain of mustard seed, ye shall say unto this mountain, Remove hence to yonder place; and it shall remove; and nothing shall be impossible unto you." Hebrews 11:32–35 and the following verses: "And what shall I more say? for the time would fail me to tell of Gideon, and of Barak, and of Samson, and of Jephthah, of David also, and Samuel, and of the prophets: who through faith subdued kingdoms, wrought righteousness, obtained promises, stopped the mouths of lions, quenched the violence of fire, escaped the edge of the sword, out of weakness were made strong, waxed valiant in fight, turned to flight the armies of the aliens. Women received their dead raised to life again, and others were tortured, not accepting deliverance; that they might obtain a better resurrection," (Lecture 1:16–22).

36. How would you define faith in its most unlimited sense?

It is the first great governing principle which has power, dominion, and authority over all things (Lecture 1:24).

37. How do you convey to the understanding more clearly that faith is the first great governing principle which has power, dominion, and authority over all things?

By it they exist, by it they are upheld, by it they are changed, or by it they remain, agreeable to the will of God; and without it there is no power, and without power there could be no creation nor existence (Lecture 1:24)!

Lecture Second

1. Having shown in our previous lecture "faith itself—what it is," we shall proceed to show, secondly, the object on which it rests.

2. We here observe that God is the only supreme governor and independent being in whom all fullness and perfection dwell; who is omnipotent, omnipresent, and omniscient; without beginning of days or end of life; and that in him every good gift and every good principle dwell; and that he is the Father of lights; in him the principle of faith dwells independently, and he is the object in whom the faith of all other rational and accountable beings center for life and salvation.

3. In order to present this part of the subject in a clear and conspicuous point of light, it is necessary to go back and show the evidences which mankind have had, and the foundation on which these evidences are, or were, based since the creation, to believe in the existence of a God.

4. We do not mean those evidences which are manifested by the works of creation which we daily behold with our natural eyes. We are sensible that, after a revelation of Jesus Christ, the works of creation, throughout their vast forms and varieties, clearly exhibit his eternal power and Godhead. Romans 1:20: "For the invisible things of him from the creation of the world are clearly seen, being understood by the things that are made, even his eternal power and Godhead"; but we mean those evidences by which the first thoughts were suggested to the minds of men that there was a God who created all things.

5. We shall now proceed to examine the situation of man at his first creation. Moses, the historian, has given us the

following account of him in the first chapter of the book of Genesis, beginning with the twentieth verse, and closing with the thirtieth. (JST Genesis 1:27–31; Moses 2:26–29). We copy from the new translation:

6. "And I, God, said unto mine Only Begotten, which was with me from the beginning, Let us make man in our image, after our likeness; and it was so.

7. "And I, God, said, Let them have dominion over the fishes of the sea, and over the fowl of the air, and over the cattle, and over all the earth, and over every creeping thing that creepeth upon the earth.

8. "And I, God, created man in mine own image, in the image of mine Only Begotten created I him; male and female created I them. And I, God, blessed them, and said unto them, Be fruitful, and multiply, and replenish the earth, and subdue it; and have dominion over the fish of the sea, and over the fowl of the air, and over every living thing that moveth upon the earth.

9. "And I, God, said unto man, Behold, I have given you every herb, bearing seed, which is upon the face of all the earth, and every tree in the which shall be the fruit of a tree, yielding seed; to you it shall be for meat."

10. Again, Genesis 2:15–17, 19–20 (JST Genesis 2:18–22, 25–27; Moses 3:15–17, 19–20): "And I, the Lord God, took the man, and put him into the garden of Eden, to dress it, and to keep it. And I, the Lord God, commanded the man, saying, Of every tree of the garden thou mayest freely eat; but of the tree of the knowledge of good and evil, thou shalt not eat of it; nevertheless thou mayest choose for thyself, for it is given unto thee; but remember that I forbid it; for in the day thou eatest thereof thou shalt surely die. . . .

11. "And out of the ground, I, the Lord God, formed every beast of the field, and every fowl of the air; and commanded that they should come unto Adam, to see what he would call them. And . . . whatsoever Adam called every living creature, that should be the name thereof. And Adam gave names to all cattle, and to the fowl of the air, and to every beast of the field."

12. From the foregoing we learn man's situation at his first creation, the knowledge with which he was endowed, and the high and exalted station in which he was placed—lord or governor of all things on earth, and at the same time enjoying communion and intercourse with his Maker, without a veil to separate between. We shall next proceed to examine the account given of his fall, and of his being driven out of the garden of Eden, and from the presence of the Lord.

13. Moses proceeds: "And they [Adam and Eve] heard the voice of the Lord God, as they were walking in the garden, in the cool of the day. And Adam and his wife went to hide themselves from the presence of the Lord God, amongst the trees of the garden. And I, the Lord God, called unto Adam, and said unto him, Where goest thou? And he said, I heard thy voice, in the garden, and I was afraid, because I beheld that I was naked, and I hid myself.

14. "And I, the Lord God, said unto Adam, Who told thee that thou wast naked? Hast thou eaten of the tree whereof I commanded thee that thou shouldst not eat, if so, thou shouldst surely die? And the man said, The woman whom thou gavest me, and commanded that she should remain with me, gave me of the fruit of the tree, and I did eat.

15. "And I, the Lord God, said unto the woman, What is this thing which thou hast done? And the woman said, The serpent beguiled me, and I did eat," (JST Genesis 3:13–19; Moses 4:14–19).

16. And again, the Lord said unto the woman, "I will greatly multiply thy sorrow, and thy conception; in sorrow thou shalt bring forth children, and thy desire shall be to thy husband, and he shall rule over thee.

17. "And unto Adam, I, the Lord God, said, Because thou hast hearkened unto the voice of thy wife, and hast eaten of the fruit of the tree, of which I commanded thee, saying, Thou shalt not eat of it, cursed shall be the ground for thy sake; in sorrow shalt thou eat of it all the days of thy life; thorns also and thistles shall it bring forth to thee; and thou shalt eat the

herb of the field; by the sweat of thy face shalt thou eat bread, until thou shalt return unto the ground, for thou shalt surely die; for out of it wast thou taken, for dust thou wast, and unto dust shalt thou return," (JST Genesis 3:22–25; Moses 4:22–25). This was immediately followed by the fulfillment of what was previously said—Man was driven or sent out of Eden.

18. Two important items are shown from the former quotations. First, after man was created, he was not left without intelligence or understanding, to wander in darkness and spend an existence in ignorance and doubt (on the great and important point which affected his happiness) as to the real fact by whom he was created, or unto whom he was amenable for his conduct. God conversed with him face to face. In his presence he was permitted to stand, and from his own mouth he was permitted to receive instruction. He heard his voice, walked before him and gazed upon his glory, while intelligence burst upon his understanding, and enabled him to give names to the vast assemblage of his Maker's works.

19. Secondly, we have seen, that though man did transgress, his transgression did not deprive him of the previous knowledge with which he was endowed relative to the existence and glory of his Creator; for no sooner did he hear his voice than he sought to hide himself from his presence.

20. Having shown, then, in the first instance, that God began to converse with man immediately after he "breathed into his nostrils the breath of life," and that he did not cease to manifest himself to him, even after his fall, we shall next proceed to show, that though he was cast out from the garden of Eden, his knowledge of the existence of God was not lost, neither did God cease to manifest his will unto him.

21. We next proceed to present the account of the direct revelation which man received after he was cast out of Eden, and further copy from the new translation:

22. After Adam had been driven out of the garden, he "began to till the earth, and to have dominion over all the beasts of the field, and to eat his bread by the sweat of his brow, as I,

the Lord had commanded him." And he called upon the name of the Lord, and so did Eve, his wife, also. "And they heard the voice of the Lord, from the way towards the garden of Eden, speaking unto them, and they saw him not; for they were shut out from his presence. And he gave unto them commandments, that they should worship the Lord their God; and should offer the firstlings of their flocks for an offering unto the Lord. And Adam was obedient unto the commandments of the Lord.

23. "And after many days, an angel of the Lord appeared unto Adam, saying, Why dost thou offer sacrifices unto the Lord? And Adam said unto him, I know not, save the Lord commanded me.

24. "And then the angel spake, saying, This thing is a similitude of the sacrifice of the Only Begotten of the Father, which is full of grace and truth; wherefore, thou shalt do all that thou doest, in the name of the Son. And thou shalt repent, and call upon God, in the name of the Son for evermore. And in that day, the Holy Ghost fell upon Adam, which beareth record of the Father and the Son," (JST Genesis 4:1, 4–9; Moses 5:1, 4–9).

25. This last quotation, or summary, shows this important fact, that though our first parents were driven out of the garden of Eden and were even separated from the presence of God by a veil, they still retained a knowledge of his existence, and that sufficiently to move them to call upon him. And further, that no sooner was the plan of redemption revealed to man, and he began to call upon God, than the Holy Spirit was given, bearing record of the Father and Son.

26. Moses also gives us an account, in the fourth chapter of Genesis, of the transgression of Cain, and the righteousness of Abel, and of the revelations of God to them, (JST Genesis 5:6–9, 17–25; Moses 5:19–23, 32–40). He says, "In process of time . . . Cain brought of the fruit of the ground an offering unto the Lord. And Abel, he also brought, of the firstlings of his flock, and of the fat thereof; and the Lord had respect unto Abel, and to his offering, but unto Cain, and to his offering he had not respect. Now Satan knew this, and it pleased him. And

Cain was very wroth, and his countenance fell. And the Lord said unto Cain, Why art thou wroth? Why is thy countenance fallen? If thou doest well thou shalt be accepted, and if thou doest not well, sin lieth at the door; and Satan desireth to have thee, and except thou shalt hearken unto my commandments, I will deliver thee up, and it shall be unto thee according to his desire. . . .

27. "And Cain went into the field, and Cain talked with Abel his brother; and it came to pass, that while they were in the field Cain rose up against Abel his brother, and slew him. And Cain gloried in that which he had done, saying, I am free; surely the flocks of my brother falleth into my hands.

28. "And the Lord said unto Cain, Where is Abel, thy brother? And he said, I know not, am I my brother's keeper? And the Lord said, What hast thou done? The voice of thy brother's blood cries unto me from the ground. And now, thou shalt be cursed from the earth, which hath opened her mouth to receive thy brother's blood from thy hand. When thou tillest the ground, it shall not henceforth yield unto thee her strength; a fugitive and a vagabond shalt thou be in the earth.

29. "And Cain said unto the Lord, Satan tempted me, because of my brother's flocks; and I was wroth also, for his offering thou didst accept, and not mine. My punishment is greater than I can bear. Behold, thou hast driven me out this day from the face of the Lord, and from thy face shall I be hid; and I shall be a fugitive and a vagabond in the earth; and it shall come to pass, that he that findeth me shall slay me, because of mine iniquities, for these things are not hid from the Lord. And I, the Lord, said unto him, Whosoever slayeth thee, vengeance shall be taken on him seven-fold; and I, the Lord, set a mark upon Cain, lest any finding him should kill him."

30. The object of the foregoing quotations is to show to this class the way by which mankind were first made acquainted with the existence of a God; that it was by a manifestation of God to man, and that God continued, after man's transgression, to manifest himself to him and to his posterity; and, notwithstanding

they were separated from his immediate presence that they could not see his face, they continued to hear his voice.

31. Adam, thus being made acquainted with God, communicated the knowledge which he had unto his posterity; and it was through this means that the thought was first suggested to their minds that there was a God, which laid the foundation for the exercise of their faith, through which they could obtain a knowledge of his character and also of his glory.

32. Not only was there a manifestation made unto Adam of the existence of a God; but Moses informs us, as before quoted, that God condescended to talk with Cain after his great transgression in slaying his brother, and that Cain knew that it was the Lord that was talking with him, so that when he was driven out from the presence of his brethren, he carried with him the knowledge of the existence of a God; and, through this means, doubtless, his posterity became acquainted with the fact that such a being existed.

33. From this we can see that the whole human family in the early age of their existence, in all their different branches, had this knowledge disseminated among them; so that the existence of God became an object of faith in the early age of the world. And the evidences which these men had of the existence of a God was the testimony of their fathers in the first instance.

34. The reason why we have been thus particular on this part of our subject is that this class may see by what means it was that God became an object of faith among men after the fall; and what it was that stirred up the faith of multitudes to feel after him—to search after a knowledge of his character, perfections, and attributes, until they became extensively acquainted with him, and not only commune with him and behold his glory, but be partakers of his power and stand in his presence.

35. Let this class mark particularly, that the testimony which these men had of the existence of a God was the testimony of man; for previous to the time that any of Adam's posterity had obtained a manifestation of God to themselves,

Adam, their common father, had testified unto them of the existence of God, and of his eternal power and Godhead.

36. For instance, Abel, before he received the assurance from heaven that his offerings were acceptable unto God, had received the important information of his father that such a being did exist, who had created and who did uphold all things. Neither can there be a doubt existing on the mind of any person, that Adam was the first who did communicate the knowledge of the existence of a God to his posterity; and that the whole faith of the world, from that time down to the present is in a certain degree dependent on the knowledge first communicated to them by their common progenitor; and it has been handed down to the day and generation in which we live, as we shall show from the face of the sacred records.

37. First, Adam was 130 years old when Seth was born (Genesis 5:3). And the days of Adam, after he had begotten Seth, were 800 years, making him 930 years old when he died (Genesis 5:4–5). Seth was 105 when Enos was born (v. 6); Enos was 90 when Cainan was born (v. 9); Cainan was 70 when Mahalaleel was born (v.12); Mahalaleel was 65 when Jared was born (v. 15); Jared was 162 when Enoch was born (v. 18); Enoch was 65 when Methuselah was born (v. 21); Methuselah was 187 when Lamech was born (v. 25); Lamech was 182 when Noah was born (v. 28).

38. From this account it appears that Lamech, the ninth from Adam, and the father of Noah, was 56 years old when Adam died; Methuselah, 243; Enoch, 308; Jared, 470; Mahalaleel, 535; Cainan, 605; Enos, 695; and Seth, 800.

39. So that Lamech (the father of Noah), Methuselah, Enoch, Jared, Mahalaleel, Cainan, Enos, Seth, and Adam were all living at the same time, and, beyond all controversy, were all preachers of righteousness.

40. Moses further informs us that Seth lived after he begat Enos, 807 years, making him 912 years old at his death (Gen. 5:7–8). And Enos lived after he begat Cainan, 815 years, making him 905 years old when he died (Gen. 5:10–11). And

Cainan lived after he begat Mahalaleel, 840 years, making him 910 years old at his death (Gen. 5:13–14). And Mahalaleel lived after he begat Jared, 830 years, making him 895 years old when he died (Gen. 5:16–17). And Jared lived after he begat Enoch, 800 years, making him 962 years old at his death (Gen. 5:19–20). And Enoch walked with God after he begat Methuselah 300 years, making him 365 years old when he was translated (Gen. 5:22–23). And Methuselah lived after he begat Lamech, 782 years, making him 969 years old when he died (Gen. 5:26–27). Lamech lived after he begat Noah, 595 years, making him 777 years old when he died (Gen. 5:30–31).

41. Agreeable to this account, Adam died in the 930th year of the world; Enoch was translated in the 987th. Seth died in the 1,042nd; Enos in the 1,140th; Cainan in the 1,235th; Mahalaleel in the 1,290th; Jared in the 1,422nd; Lamech in the 1,651st; and Methuselah in the 1,656th, it being the same year in which the flood came.

42. So that Noah was 84 years old when Enos died, 176 when Cainan died, 234 when Mahalaleel died, 366 when Jared died, 595 when Lamech died, and 600 when Methuselah died.

43. We can see from this that Enos, Cainan, Mahalaleel, Jared, Methuselah, Lamech, and Noah all lived on the earth at the same time; and that Enos, Cainan, Mahalaleel, Jared, Methuselah, and Lamech were all acquainted with both Adam and Noah.

44. From the foregoing it is easily to be seen, not only how the knowledge of God came into the world, but upon what principle it was preserved; that from the time it was first communicated, it was retained in the minds of righteous men, who taught not only their own posterity but the world; so that there was no need of a new revelation to man, after Adam's creation to Noah, to give them the first idea or notion of the existence of a God; and not only of a God, but the true and living God.

45. Having traced the chronology of the world from Adam to Noah, we will now trace it from Noah to Abraham. Noah

was 502 years old when Shem was born; 98 years afterwards the flood came, being the 600th year of Noah's age. And Moses informs us that Noah lived after the flood 350 years, making him 950 years old when he died (Gen. 9:28–29).

46. Shem was 100 years old when Arphaxad was born (Gen. 11:10). Arphaxad was 35 when Salah was born (11:12); Salah was 30 when Eber was born (11:14); Eber was 34 when Peleg was born, in whose days the earth was divided (11:16); Peleg was 30 when Reu was born (11:18); Reu was 32 when Serug was born (11:20); Serug was 30 when Nahor was born (11:22); Nahor was 29 when Terah was born (11:24); Terah was 70 when Haran and Abraham were born (11:26).

47. There is some difficulty in the account given by Moses of Abraham's birth. Some have supposed that Abraham was not born until Terah was 130 years old. This conclusion is drawn from a variety of scriptures, which are not to our purpose at present to quote. Neither is it a matter of any consequence to us whether Abraham was born when Terah was 70 years old, or 130. But in order that there may no doubt exist upon any mind in relation to the object lying immediately before us, in presenting the present chronology we will date the birth of Abraham at the latest period, that is, when Terah was 130 years old. It appears from this account that from the flood to the birth of Abraham was 352 years.

48. Moses informs us that Shem lived after he begat Arphaxad, 500 years (Gen. 11:11); this added to 100 years, which was his age when Arphaxad was born, makes him 600 years old when he died. Arphaxad lived after he begat Salah, 403 years (11:13); this added to 35 years, which was his age when Salah was born, makes him 438 years old when he died. Salah lived after he begat Eber, 403 years (11:15); this added to 30 years, which was his age when Eber was born, makes him 433 years old when he died. Eber lived after he begat Peleg, 430 years (11:17); this added to 34 years, which was his age when Peleg was born, makes him 464 years old. Peleg lived after he begat Reu, 209 years (11:19); this added to 30 years, which was

his age when Reu was born, makes him 239 years old when he died. Reu lived after he begat Serug 207 years (11:21); this added to 32 years, which was his age when Serug was born, makes him 239 years old when he died. Serug lived after he begat Nahor, 200 years (11:23); this added to 30 years, which was his age when Nahor was born, makes him 230 years old when he died. Nahor lived after he begat Terah, 119 years (11:25); this added to 29 years, which was his age when Terah was born, makes him 148 years old when he died. Terah was 130 years old when Abraham was born, and is supposed to have lived 75 years after his birth, making him 205 years old when he died.

49. Agreeable to this last account, Peleg died in the 1,996th year of the world, Nahor in the 1,997th, and Noah in the 2,006th. So that Peleg, in whose days the earth was divided, and Nahor, the grandfather of Abraham, both died before Noah—the former being 239 years old, and the latter 148; and who cannot but see that they must have had a long and intimate acquaintance with Noah?

50. Reu died in the 2,026th year of the world, Serug in the 2,049th, Terah in the 2,083rd, Arphaxad in the 2,096th, Salah in the 2,126th, Shem in the 2,158th, Abraham in the 2,183rd, and Eber in the 2,187th, which was four years after Abraham's death. And Eber was the fourth from Noah.

51. Nahor, Abraham's brother, was 58 years old when Noah died; Terah, 128; Serug, 187; Reu, 219; Eber, 283; Salah, 313; Arphaxad, 344; and Shem, 448.

52. It appears from this account, that Nahor, brother of Abraham, Terah, Nahor, Serug, Reu, Peleg, Eber, Salah, Arphaxad, Shem, and Noah all lived on the earth at the same time; and that Abraham was 18 years old when Reu died, 41 when Serug and his brother Nahor died, 75 when Terah died, 88 when Arphaxad died, 118 when Salah died, 150 when Shem died, and that Eber lived four years after Abraham's death. And that Shem, Arphaxad, Salah, Eber, Reu, Serug, Terah, and Nahor, the brother of Abraham, and Abraham lived at the same

time. And that Nahor, brother of Abraham, Terah, Serug, Reu, Eber, Salah, Arphaxad, and Shem were all acquainted with both Noah and Abraham.

53. We have now traced the chronology of the world agreeable to the account given in our present Bible, from Adam to Abraham, and have clearly determined, beyond the power of controversy, that there was no difficulty in preserving the knowledge of God in the world from the creation of Adam, and the manifestation made to his immediate descendants, as set forth in the former part of this lecture; so that the students in this class need not have any doubt resting on their minds on this subject, for they can easily see that it is impossible for it to be otherwise, but that the knowledge of the existence of a God must have continued from father to son, as a matter of tradition at least; for we cannot suppose that a knowledge of this important fact could have existed in the mind of any of the before-mentioned individuals, without their having made it known to their posterity.

54. We have now shown how it was that the first thought ever existed in the mind of any individual that there was such a being as a God, who had created and did uphold all things: that it was by reason of the manifestation which he first made to our father Adam, when he stood in his presence, and conversed with him face to face, at the time of his creation.

55. Let us here observe, that after any portion of the human family are made acquainted with the important fact that there is a God, who has created and does uphold all things, the extent of their knowledge respecting his character and glory will depend upon their diligence and faithfulness in seeking after him, until, like Enoch, the brother of Jared, and Moses, they shall obtain faith in God, and power with him to behold him face to face.

56. We have now clearly set forth how it is, and how it was, that God became an object of faith for rational beings; and also, upon what foundation the testimony was based which excited the inquiry and diligent search of the ancient saints to seek after

and obtain a knowledge of the glory of God; and we have seen that it was human testimony, and human testimony only, that excited this inquiry, in the first instance, in their minds. It was the credence they gave to the testimony of their fathers, this testimony having aroused their minds to inquire after the knowledge of God; the inquiry frequently terminated, indeed always terminated when rightly pursued, in the most glorious discoveries and eternal certainty.

QUESTIONS AND ANSWERS ON THE FOREGOING PRINCIPLES

57. Is there a being who has faith in himself, independently?
There is.

58. Who is it?
It is God.

59. How do you prove that God has faith in himself independently?
Because he is omnipotent, omnipresent, and omniscient, without beginning of days or end of life, and in him all fullness dwells. Ephesians 1:23: "Which is his body, the fulness of him that filleth all in all." Colossians 1:19: "For it pleased the Father that in him should all fulness dwell," (Lecture 2:2).

60. Is he the object in whom the faith of all other rational and accountable beings center, for life and salvation?
He is.

61. How do you prove it?
Isaiah 45:22: "Look unto me, and be ye saved, all the ends of the earth: for I am God, and there is none else." Romans 11:34–36: "For who hath known the mind of the Lord? Or who hath been his counsellor? Or who hath first given to him, and it shall be recompensed unto him again? For of him, and through him, and to him, are all things: to whom be glory for

ever. Amen." Isaiah 40, from the ninth to the eighteenth verses: "O Zion, that bringest good tidings [or, O thou that tellest good tidings to Zion], get thee up into the high mountain; O Jerusalem, that bringest good tidings [or, O thou that tellest good tidings to Jerusalem], lift up thy voice with strength; lift it up, be not afraid; say unto the cities of Judah, Behold your God! Behold, the Lord God will come with strong hand [or, against the strong], and his arm shall rule for him: behold, his reward is with him, and his work before him [or, recompense for his work]. He shall feed his flock like a shepherd: he shall gather the lambs with his arm, and carry them in his bosom, and shall gently lead those that are with young. Who hath measured the waters in the hollow of his hand, and meted out heaven with the span, and comprehended the dust of the earth in a measure, and weighed the mountains in scales, and the hills in a balance? Who hath directed the Spirit of the Lord, or being his counsellor hath taught him? With whom took he counsel, and who instructed him, and taught him in the path of judgment, and taught him knowledge, and shewed to him the way of understanding? Behold, the nations are as a drop of a bucket, and are counted as the small dust of the balance: behold, he taketh up the isles as a very little thing. And Lebanon is not sufficient to burn, nor the beasts thereof sufficient for a burnt offering. All nations before him are as nothing; and they are counted to him less than nothing, and vanity." Jeremiah 51:15–16: "He [the Lord] hath made the earth by his power, he hath established the world by his wisdom, and hath stretched out the heaven by his understanding. When he uttereth his voice, there is a multitude of waters in the heavens; and he causeth the vapours to ascend from the ends of the earth: he maketh lightnings with rain, and bringeth forth the wind out of his treasures." 1 Corinthians 8:6: "But to us there is but one God, the Father, of whom are all things, and we in him; and one Lord Jesus Christ, by whom are all things, and we by him," (Lecture 2:2).

62. How did men first come to the knowledge of the existence of a God, so as to exercise faith in him?

In order to answer this question, it will be necessary to go back and examine man at his creation, the circumstances in which he was placed, and the knowledge which he had of God (Lecture 2:3–11). First, when man was created he stood in the presence of God (Gen. 1:27–28). From this we learn that man, at his creation, stood in the presence of his God, and had most perfect knowledge of his existence. Secondly, God conversed with him after his transgression (Gen. 3:8–22; Lecture 2:13–17). From this we learn that, though man did transgress, he was not deprived of the previous knowledge which he had of the existence of God (Lecture 2:19). Thirdly, God conversed with man after he cast him out of the garden (Lecture 2:22–25). Fourthly, God also conversed with Cain after he had slain Abel (Gen. 4:4–6; Lecture 2:26–29).

63. What is the object of the foregoing quotation?

It is that it may be clearly seen how it was that the first thoughts were suggested to the minds of men of the existence of God, and how extensively this knowledge was spread among the immediate descendants of Adam (Lecture 2:30–33).

64. What testimony had the immediate descendants of Adam, in proof of the existence of God?

The testimony of their father. And after they were made acquainted with his existence, by the testimony of their father, they were dependent upon the exercise of their own faith, for a knowledge of his character, perfections, and attributes (Lecture 2:23–26).

65. Had any other of the human family, besides Adam, a knowledge of the existence of God, in the first instance, by any other means than human testimony?

They had not. For previous to the time that they could have power to obtain a manifestation for themselves, the all-important fact had been communicated to them by their common father; and so from father to child the knowledge was communicated as extensively as the knowledge of his existence was known; for it was by this means, in the first instance, that men had a knowledge of his existence (Lecture 2:35–36).

66. How do you know that the knowledge of the existence of God was communicated in this manner, throughout the different ages of the world?
   By the chronology obtained through the revelations of God.

67. How would you divide that chronology in order to convey it to the understanding clearly?
   Into two parts—First, by embracing that period of the world from Adam to Noah; and secondly, from Noah to Abraham; from which period the knowledge of the existence of God has been so general, that it is a matter of no dispute in what manner the idea of his existence has been retained in the world.

68. How many noted righteous men lived from Adam to Noah?
   Nine—which includes Abel, who was slain by his brother.

69. What are their names?
   Abel, Seth, Enos, Cainan, Mahalaleel, Jared, Enoch, Methuselah, and Lamech.

70. How old was Adam when Seth was born?
   One hundred and thirty years (Gen. 5:3).

71. How many years did Adam live after Seth was born?
   Eight hundred (Gen. 5:4).

72. How old was Adam when he died?
   Nine hundred and thirty years (Gen. 5:5).

73. How old was Seth when Enos was born?
One hundred and five years (Gen. 5:6).

74. How old was Enos when Cainan was born?
Ninety years (Gen. 5:9).

75. How old was Cainan when Mahalaleel was born?
Seventy years (Gen. 5:12).

76. How old was Mahalaleel when Jared was born?
Sixty-five years (Gen. 5:15).

77. How old was Jared when Enoch was born?
One hundred and sixty-two years (Gen. 5:18).

78. How old was Enoch when Methuselah was born?
Sixty-five years (Gen. 5:21).

79. How old was Methuselah when Lamech was born?
One hundred and eighty-seven years (Gen. 5:25).

80. How old was Lamech when Noah was born?
One hundred and eighty-two years (Gen. 5:28). For this chronology, see Lecture 2:37.

81. How many years, according to this account, was it from Adam to Noah?
One thousand and fifty-six years.

82. How old was Lamech when Adam died?
Lamech, the ninth from Adam (including Abel), and father of Noah, was fifty-six years old when Adam died.

83. How old was Methuselah?
Two hundred and forty-three years.

84. How old was Enoch?
Three hundred and eight years.

85. How old was Jared?
Four hundred and seventy years.

86. How old was Mahalaleel?
Five hundred and thirty-five years.

87. How old was Cainan?
Six hundred and five years.

88. How old was Enos?
Six hundred and ninety-five years.

89. How old was Seth?
Eight hundred years. For this item of the account, see
Lecture 2:38.

90. How many of these noted men were contemporary with Adam?
Nine.

91. What are their names?
Abel, Seth, Enos, Cainan, Mahalaleel, Jared, Enoch,
Methuselah, and Lamech (Lecture 2:39).

92. How long did Seth live after Enos was born?
Eight hundred and seven years (Gen. 5:7).

93. What was Seth's age when he died?
Nine hundred and twelve years (Gen. 5:8).

94. How long did Enos live after Cainan was born?
Eight hundred and fifteen years (Gen. 5:10).

95. *What was Enos's age when he died?*
Nine hundred and five years (Gen. 5:11).

96. *How long did Cainan live after Mahalaleel was born?*
Eight hundred and forty years (Gen. 5:13).

97. *What was Cainan's age when he died?*
Nine hundred and ten years (Gen. 5:14).

98. *How long did Mahalaleel live after Jared was born?*
Eight hundred and thirty years (Gen. 5:16).

99. *What was Mahalaleel's age when he died?*
Eight hundred and ninety-five years (Gen. 5:17).

100. *How long did Jared live after Enoch was born?*
Eight hundred years (Gen. 5:19).

101. *What was Jared's age when he died?*
Nine hundred and sixty-two years (Gen. 5:20).

102. *How long did Enoch walk with God after Methuselah was born?*
Three hundred years (Gen. 5:22).

103. *What was Enoch's age when he was translated?*
Three hundred and sixty-five years (Gen. 5:23).

104. *How long did Methuselah live after Lamech was born?*
Seven hundred and eighty-two years (Gen. 5:26).

105. *What was Methuselah's age when he died?*
Nine hundred and sixty-nine years (Gen. 5:27).

106. *How long did Lamech live after Noah was born?*
Five hundred and ninety-five years (Gen. 5:30).

107. What was Lamech's age when he died?
Seven hundred and seventy-seven years (Gen. 5:31). For the account of the last item, see Lecture 2:40.

108. In what year of the world did Adam die?
In the nine hundred and thirtieth.

109. In what year was Enoch translated?
In the nine hundred and eighty-seventh.

110. In what year did Seth die?
In the one thousand and forty-second.

111. In what year did Enos die?
In the eleven hundred and fortieth.

112. In what year did Cainan die?
In the twelve hundred and thirty-fifth.

113. In what year did Mahalaleel die?
In the twelve hundred and ninetieth.

114. In what year did Jared die?
In the fourteen hundred and twenty-second.

115. In what year did Lamech die?
In the sixteen hundred and fifty-first.

116. In what year did Methuselah die?
In the sixteen hundred and fifty-sixth. For this account, see Lecture 2:41.

117. How old was Noah when Enos died?
Eighty-four years.

118. How old when Cainan died?
One hundred and seventy-nine years.

119. How old when Mahalaleel died?
Two hundred and thirty-four years.

120. How old when Jared died?
Three hundred and sixty-six years.

121. How old when Lamech died?
Five hundred and ninety-five years.

122. How old when Methuselah died?
Six hundred years. See Lecture 2:42 for the last item.

123. How many of those men lived in the days of Noah?
Six.

124. What are their names?
Enos, Cainan, Mahalaleel, Jared, Methuselah, and Lamech (Lecture 2:43).

125. How many of those men were contemporary with Adam and Noah both?
Six.

126. What are their names?
Enos, Cainan, Mahalaleel, Jared, Methuselah, and Lamech (Lecture 2:43).

127. According to the foregoing account, how was the knowledge of the existence of God first suggested to the minds of men?
By the manifestation made to our father Adam, when he was in the presence of God, both before and while he was in Eden (Lecture 2:44).

128. How was the knowledge of the existence of God disseminated among the inhabitants of the world?
By tradition from father to son (Lecture 2:44).

129. How old was Noah when Shem was born?
Five hundred and two years (Gen. 5:32).

130. What was the term of years from the birth of Shem to the flood?
Ninety-eight.

131. What was the term of years that Noah lived after the flood?
Three hundred and fifty (Gen. 9:28).

132. What was Noah's age when he died?
Nine hundred and fifty years (Gen. 9:29; Lecture 2:45).

133. What was Shem's age when Arphaxad was born?
One hundred years (Gen. 11:10).

134. What was Arphaxad's age when Salah was born?
Thirty-five years (Gen. 11:12).

135. What was Salah's age when Eber was born?
Thirty years (Gen. 11:14).

136. What was Eber's age when Peleg was born?
Thirty-four years (Gen. 11:16).

137. What was Peleg's age when Reu was born?
Thirty years (Gen. 11:18).

138. What was Reu's age when Serug was born?
Thirty-two years (Gen. 11:20).

139. What was Serug's age when Nahor was born?
Thirty years (Gen. 11:22).

140. What was Nahor's age when Terah was born?
Twenty-nine years (Gen. 11:24).

141. What was Terah's age when Nahor (the [brother] of Abraham) was born?
Seventy years (Gen. 11:26).

142. What was Terah's age when Abraham was born?
Some suppose one hundred and thirty years, and others seventy (Gen. 11:26; Lecture 2:46).

143. What was the number of years from the flood to the birth of Abraham?
Supposing Abraham to have been born when Terah was one hundred and thirty years old, it was three hundred and fifty-two years: but if he was born when Terah was seventy years old, it was two hundred and ninety-two years (Lecture 2:47).

144. How long did Shem live after Arphaxad was born?
Five hundred years (Gen. 11:11).

145. What was Shem's age when he died?
Six hundred years (Gen. 11:11).

146. What number of years did Arphaxad live after Salah was born?
Four hundred and three years (Gen. 11:13).

147. What was Arphaxad's age when he died?
Four hundred and thirty-eight years.

148. What number of years did Salah live after Eber was born?
Four hundred and three years.

149. What was Salah's age when he died?
Four hundred and thirty-three years.

150. What number of years did Eber live after Peleg was born?
Four hundred and thirty years (Gen. 11:17).

151. What was Eber's age when he died?
Four hundred and sixty-four years.

152. What number of years did Peleg live after Reu was born?
Two hundred and nine years (Gen. 11:19).

153. What was Peleg's age when he died?
Two hundred and thirty-nine years.

154. What number of years did Reu live after Serug was born?
Two hundred and seven years (Gen. 11:21).

155. What was Reu's age when he died?
Two hundred and thirty-nine years.

156. What number of years did Serug live after Nahor was born?
Two hundred years (Gen. 11:23).

157. What was Serug's age when he died?
Two hundred and thirty years.

158. What number of years did Nahor live after Terah was born?
One hundred and nineteen years (Gen. 11:25).

159. What was Nahor's age when he died?
One hundred and forty-eight years.

160. What number of years did Terah live after Abraham was born?
Supposing Terah to have been one hundred and thirty years old when Abraham was born, he lived seventy-five years; but if Abraham was born when Terah was seventy years old, he lived one hundred and thirty-five years.

161. What was Terah's age when he died?

Two hundred and five years (Gen. 11:32). For this account from the birth of Arphaxad to the death of Terah, see Lecture 2:48.

162. In what year of the world did Peleg die?

Agreeable to the foregoing chronology, he died in the nineteen hundred and ninety-sixth year of the world.

163. In what year of the world did Nahor die?

In the nineteen hundred and ninety-seventh.

164. In what year of the world did Noah die?

In the two thousand and sixth.

165. In what year of the world did Reu die?

In the two thousand and twenty-sixth.

166. In what year of the world did Serug die?

In the two thousand and forty-ninth.

167. In what year of the world did Terah die?

In the two thousand and eighty-third.

168. In what year of the world did Arphaxad die?

In the two thousand and ninety-sixth.

169. In what year of the world did Salah die?

In the twenty-one hundred and twenty-sixth.

170. In what year of the world did Abraham die?

In the twenty-one hundred and eighty-third.

171. In what year of the world did Eber die?

In the twenty-one hundred and eighty-seventh. For this account of the year of the world in which those men died, see Lecture 2:49–50.

172. How old was Nahor (Abraham's brother) when Noah died?
Fifty-eight years.

173. How old was Terah?
One hundred and twenty-eight.

174. How old was Serug?
One hundred and eighty-seven.

175. How old was Reu?
Two hundred and nineteen.

176. How old was Eber?
Two hundred and eighty-three.

177. How old was Salah?
Three hundred and thirteen.

178. How old was Arphaxad?
Three hundred and forty-eight.

179. How old was Shem?
Four hundred and forty-eight. For the last account, see Lecture 2:51.

180. How old was Abraham when Reu died?
Eighteen years, if he was born when Terah was one hundred and thirty years old.

181. What was his age when Serug and Nahor (Abraham's brother) died?
Forty-one years.

182. What was his age when Terah died?
Seventy-five years.

183. What was his age when Arphaxad died?
Eighty-eight.

184. What was his age when Salah died?
One hundred and eighteen years.

185. What was his age when Shem died?
One hundred and fifty years. For this, see Lecture 2:52.

186. How many noted characters lived from Noah to Abraham?
Ten.

187. What are their names?
Shem, Arphaxad, Salah, Eber, Peleg, Reu, Serug, Nahor, Terah, and Abraham's brother, Nahor (Lecture 2:52).

188. How many of these were contemporary with Noah?
The whole.

189. How many with Abraham?
Eight.

190. What are their names?
Nahor (Abraham's brother), Terah, Serug, Reu, Eber, Salah, Arphaxad, and Shem (Lecture 2:52).

191. How many were contemporary with both Noah and Abraham?
Eight.

192. What are their names?
Shem, Arphaxad, Salah, Eber, Reu, Serug, Terah, and Abraham's brother, Nahor (Lecture 2:52).

193. Did any of these men die before Noah?
They did.

194. Who were they?
Peleg, in whose days the earth was divided, and Abraham's grandfather, Nahor (Lecture 2:49).

195. Did any one of them live longer than Abraham?
There was one (Lecture 2:50).

196. Who was he?
Eber, the fourth from Noah (Lecture 2:50).

197. In whose days was the earth divided?
In the days of Peleg.

198. Where have we the account given that the earth was divided in the days of Peleg?
Gen. 10:25.

199. Can you repeat the sentence?
"Unto Eber were born two sons: the name of one was Peleg; for in his days was the earth divided."

200. What testimony have men, in the first instance, that there is a God?
Human testimony, and human testimony only (Lecture 2:56).

201. What excited the ancient saints to seek diligently after a knowledge of the glory of God, his perfections, and attributes?
The credence they gave to the testimony of their fathers (Lecture 2:56).

202. How do men obtain a knowledge of the glory of God, his perfections, and attributes?
By devoting themselves to his service through prayer and supplication, incessantly strengthening their faith in him, until, like Enoch, the brother of Jared, and Moses, they obtain a manifestation of God to themselves (Lecture 2:55).

203. Is the knowledge of the existence of God a matter of mere tradition, founded upon human testimony alone, until persons receive a manifestation of God to themselves?

It is.

204. How do you prove it?

From the whole of the first and second lectures.

LECTURE THIRD

1. In the second lecture it was shown how it was that the knowledge of the existence of God came into the world, and by what means the first thoughts were suggested to the minds of men that such a being did actually exist; and that it was by reason of the knowledge of his existence that there was a foundation laid for the exercise of faith in him, as the only being in whom faith could center for life and salvation; for faith could not center in a being of whose existence we have no idea, because the idea of his existence in the first instance is essential to the exercise of faith in him. Romans 10:14: "How then shall they call on him in whom they have not believed? and how shall they believe in him of whom they have not heard? and how shall they hear without a preacher?" (or one sent to tell them?) So, then, faith comes by hearing the word of God.

2. Let us here observe, that three things are necessary in order that any rational and intelligent being may exercise faith in God unto life and salvation.

3. First, the idea that he actually exists.

4. Secondly, a correct idea of his character, perfections, and attributes.

5. Thirdly, an actual knowledge that the course of life which he is pursuing is according to his will. For without an acquaintance with these three important facts, the faith of every rational being must be imperfect and unproductive; but with this understanding it can become perfect and fruitful, abounding in righteousness, unto the praise and glory of God the Father, and the Lord Jesus Christ.

6. Having previously been made acquainted with the way the idea of his existence came into the world, as well as the fact of his existence, we shall proceed to examine his character, perfections, and attributes, in order that this class may see, not only the just grounds which they have for the exercise of faith in him for life and salvation, but the reasons that all the world, also, as far as the idea of his existence extends, may have to exercise faith in him, the Father of all living.

7. As we have been indebted to a revelation which God made of himself to his creatures, in the first instance, for the idea of his existence, so in like manner we are indebted to the revelations which he has given to us for a correct understanding of his character, perfections, and attributes; because, without the revelations which he has given to us, no man by searching could find out God (Job 11:7–9). 1 Corinthians 2:9–11: "But as it is written, Eye hath not seen, nor ear heard, neither have entered into the heart of man, the things which God hath prepared for them that love him. But God hath revealed them unto us by his Spirit: for the Spirit searcheth all things, yea, the deep things of God. For what man knoweth the things of a man, save the spirit of man which is in him? even so the things of God knoweth no man, but the Spirit of God."

8. Having said so much we proceed to examine the character which the revelations have given of God.

9. Moses gives us the following account in Exodus 34:6: "And the Lord passed by before him, and proclaimed, The Lord, the Lord God, merciful and gracious, longsuffering and abundant in goodness and truth." Psalms 103:6–8: "The Lord executeth righteousness and judgment for all that are oppressed. He made known his ways unto Moses, his acts unto the children of Israel. The Lord is merciful and gracious, slow to anger, and plenteous in mercy." Psalms 103:17–18: "But the mercy of the Lord is from everlasting to everlasting upon them that fear him, and his righteousness unto children's children; to such as keep his covenant, and to those that remember his commandments to do them." Psalm 90:2: "Before the mountains were

brought forth, or ever thou hadst formed the earth and the world, even from everlasting to everlasting, thou art God." Hebrews 1:10–12: "And, Thou, Lord, in the beginning hast laid the foundation of the earth; and the heavens are the works of thine hands: they shall perish; but thou remainest; and they all shall wax old as doth a garment; and as a vesture shalt thou fold them up, and they shall be changed: but thou art the same, and thy years shall not fail." James 1:17: "Every good gift and every perfect gift is from above, and cometh down from the Father of lights, with whom is no variableness, neither shadow of turning." Malachi 3:6: "For I am the Lord, I change not; therefore ye sons of Jacob are not consumed."

10. Book of Commandments, chapter 2, commencing in the third line of the first paragraph (D&C 3:2): "For God doth not walk in crooked paths; neither doth he turn to the right hand nor the left; neither doth he vary from that which he hath said: Therefore his paths are strait, and his course is one eternal round." Book of Commandments, chapter 37, verse 1 (D&C 35:1): "Listen to the voice of the Lord your God, even Alpha and Omega, the beginning and the end, whose course is one eternal round, the same today as yesterday and forever."

11. Numbers 23:19: "God is not a man, that he should lie; neither the son of man, that he should repent." 1 John 4:8: "He that loveth not knoweth not God; for God is love." Acts 10:34–35: "Then Peter opened his mouth, and said, Of a truth I perceive that God is no respecter of persons: but in every nation he that feareth him, and worketh righteousness is accepted with him."

12. From the foregoing testimonies we learn the following things respecting the character of God:

13. First, that he was God before the world was created, and the same God that he was after it was created.

14. Secondly, that he is merciful and gracious, slow to anger, abundant in goodness, and that he was so from everlasting, and will be to everlasting.

15. Thirdly, that he changes not, neither is there variableness with him; but that he is the same from everlasting to

everlasting, being the same yesterday, today, and forever; and that his course is one eternal round, without variation.

16. Fourthly, that he is a God of truth and cannot lie.

17. Fifthly, that he is no respecter of persons: but in every nation he that fears God and works righteousness is accepted of him.

18. Sixthly, that he is love.

19. An acquaintance with these attributes in the divine character, is essentially necessary, in order that the faith of any rational being can center in him for life and salvation. For if he did not, in the first instance, believe him to be God, that is, the Creator and upholder of all things, he could not center his faith in him for life and salvation, for fear there should be greater than he who would thwart all his plans, and he, like the gods of the heathen, would be unable to fulfill his promises; but seeing he is God over all, from everlasting to everlasting, the Creator and upholder of all things, no such fear can exist in the minds of those who put their trust in him, so that in this respect their faith can be without wavering.

20. But secondly; unless he was merciful and gracious, slow to anger, long-suffering and full of goodness, such is the weakness of human nature, and so great the frailties and imperfections of men, that unless they believed that these excellencies existed in the divine character, the faith necessary to salvation could not exist; for doubt would take the place of faith, and those who know their weakness and liability to sin would be in constant doubt of salvation if it were not for the idea which they have of the excellency of the character of God, that he is slow to anger and long-suffering, and of a forgiving disposition, and does forgive iniquity, transgression, and sin. An idea of these facts does away doubt, and makes faith exceedingly strong.

21. But it is equally as necessary that men should have the idea that he is a God who changes not, in order to have faith in him, as it is to have the idea that he is gracious and long-suffering; for without the idea of unchangeableness in the char-

acter of the Deity, doubt would take the place of faith. But with the idea that he changes not, faith lays hold upon the excellencies in his character with unshaken confidence, believing he is the same yesterday, today, and forever, and that his course is one eternal round.

22. And again, the idea that he is a God of truth and cannot lie is equally as necessary to the exercise of faith in him as the idea of his unchangeableness. For without the idea that he was a God of truth and could not lie, the confidence necessary to be placed in his word in order to the exercise of faith in him could not exist. But having the idea that he is not man, that he cannot lie, it gives power to the minds of men to exercise faith in him.

23. But it is also necessary that men should have an idea that he is no respecter of persons, for with the idea of all the other excellencies in his character, and this one wanting, men could not exercise faith in him; because if he were a respecter of persons, they could not tell what their privileges were, nor how far they were authorized to exercise faith in him, or whether they were authorized to do it at all, but all must be confusion; but no sooner are the minds of men made acquainted with the truth on this point, that he is no respecter of persons, than they see that they have authority by faith to lay hold on eternal life, the richest boon of heaven, because God is no respecter of persons, and that every man in every nation has an equal privilege.

24. And lastly, but not less important to the exercise of faith in God, is the idea that he is love; for with all the other excellencies in his character, without this one to influence them, they could not have such powerful dominion over the minds of men; but when the idea is planted in the mind that he is love, who cannot see the just ground that men of every nation, kindred, and tongue, have to exercise faith in God so as to obtain eternal life?

25. From the above description of the character of the Deity, which is given him in the revelations to men, there is a sure foundation for the exercise of faith in him among every people, nation, and kindred, from age to age, and from generation to generation.

26. Let us here observe that the foregoing is the character which is given of God in his revelations to the Former-day Saints, and it is also the character which is given of him in his revelations to the Latter-day Saints, so that the saints of former days and those of latter days are both alike in this respect; the Latter-day Saints having as good grounds to exercise faith in God as the Former-day Saints had, because the same character is given of him to both.

QUESTIONS AND ANSWERS ON THE FOREGOING PRINCIPLES

27. *What was shown in the second lecture?*

It was shown how the knowledge of the existence of God came into the world (Lecture 3:1).

28. *What is the effect of the idea of his existence among men?*

It lays the foundation for the exercise of faith in him (Lecture 3:1).

29. *Is the idea of his existence, in the first instance, necessary in order for the exercise of faith in him?*

It is (Lecture 3:1).

30. *How do you prove it?*

By the tenth chapter of Romans and fourteenth verse (Lecture 3:1).

31. *How many things are necessary for us to understand, respecting the Deity and our relation to him, in order that we may exercise faith in him for life and salvation?*

Three (Lecture 3:2).

32. *What are they?*

First, that God does actually exist; secondly, correct ideas of his character, his perfections, and attributes; and thirdly, that the course which we pursue is according to his mind and will (Lecture 3:3–5).

33. Would the idea of any one or two of the above-mentioned things enable a person to exercise faith in God?

It would not, for without the idea of them all faith would be imperfect and unproductive (Lecture 3:5).

34. Would an idea of these three things lay a sure foundation for the exercise of faith in God, so as to obtain life and salvation?

It would; for by the idea of these three things, faith could become perfect and fruitful, abounding in righteousness unto the praise and glory of God (Lecture 3:5).

35. How are we to be made acquainted with the before-mentioned things respecting the Deity, and respecting ourselves?

By revelation (Lecture 3:6).

36. Could these things be found out by any other means than by revelation?

They could not.

37. How do you prove it?

By the scriptures (Job 11:7–9; 1 Corinthians 2:9–11; Lecture 3:7).

38. What things do we learn in the revelations of God respecting his character?

We learn the six following things: First, that he was God before the world was created, and the same God that he was after it was created. Secondly, that he is merciful and gracious, slow to anger, abundant in goodness, and that he was so from everlasting, and will be so to everlasting. Thirdly, that he changes not, neither is there variableness with him, and that his course is one eternal round. Fourthly, that he is a God of truth, and cannot lie. Fifthly, that he is no respecter of persons; and sixthly, that he is love (Lecture 3:12–18).

39. Where do you find the revelations which give us this idea of the character of the Deity?

In the Bible and Book of Commandments, and they are quoted in the third lecture (Lecture 3:9-11).

40. What effect would it have on any rational being not to have an idea that the Lord was God, the Creator and upholder of all things?

It would prevent him from exercising faith in him unto life and salvation.

41. Why would it prevent him from exercising faith in God?

Because he would be as the heathen, not knowing but there might be a being greater and more powerful than he, and thereby he be prevented from fulfilling his promises (Lecture 3:19).

42. Does this idea prevent this doubt?

It does; for persons having this idea are enabled thereby to exercise faith without this doubt (Lecture 3:19).

43. Is it not also necessary to have the idea that God is merciful and gracious, long-suffering and full of goodness?

It is (Lecture 3:20).

44. Why is it necessary?

Because of the weakness and imperfections of human nature, and the great frailties of man; for such is the weakness of man, and such his frailties, that he is liable to sin continually, and if God were not long-suffering, and full of compassion, gracious and merciful, and of a forgiving disposition, man would be cut off from before him, in consequence of which he would be in continual doubt and could not exercise faith; for where doubt is, there faith has no power; but by man's believing that God is full of compassion and forgiveness, long-suffering and slow to anger, he can exercise faith in him and overcome doubt, so as to be exceedingly strong (Lecture 3:20).

45. Is it not equally as necessary that man should have an idea that God changes not, neither is there variableness with him, in order to exercise faith in him unto life and salvation?

It is; because without this, he would not know how soon the mercy of God might change into cruelty, his long-suffering into rashness, his love into hatred, and in consequence of which doubt man would be incapable of exercising faith in him, but having the idea that he is unchangeable, man can have faith in him continually, believing that what he was yesterday he is to-day, and will be forever (Lecture 3:21).

46. Is it not necessary also for men to have an idea that God is a being of truth before they can have perfect faith in him?

It is; for unless men have this idea they cannot place confidence in his word, and, not being able to place confidence in his word, they could not have faith in him; but believing that he is a God of truth, and that his word cannot fail, their faith can rest in him without doubt (Lecture 3:22).

47. Could man exercise faith in God so as to obtain eternal life unless he believed that God was no respecter of persons?

He could not, because without this idea he could not certainly know that it was his privilege so to do, and in consequence of this doubt his faith could not be sufficiently strong to save him (Lecture 3:23).

48. Would it be possible for a man to exercise faith in God, so as to be saved, unless he had an idea that God was love?

He could not; because man could not love God unless he had an idea that God was love, and if he did not love God he could not have faith in him (Lecture 3:24).

49. What is the description which the sacred writers give of the character of the Deity calculated to do?

It is calculated to lay a foundation for the exercise of faith in him, as far as the knowledge extends, among all people, tongues, languages, kindreds, and nations, and that from age to age, and from generation to generation (Lecture 3:25).

50. Is the character which God has given of himself uniform?

It is, in all his revelations, whether to the Former-day Saints, or to the Latter-day Saints, so that they all have the authority to exercise faith in him, and to expect, by the exercise of their faith, to enjoy the same blessings (Lecture 3:26).

LECTURE FOURTH

1. Having shown, in the third lecture, that correct ideas of the character of God are necessary in order to exercise faith in him unto life and salvation; and that without correct ideas of his character the minds of men could not have sufficient power with God to the exercise of faith necessary to the enjoyment of eternal life; and that correct ideas of his character lay a foundation, as far as his character is concerned, for the exercise of faith, so as to enjoy the fullness of the blessing of the gospel of Jesus Christ, even that of eternal glory; we shall now proceed to show the connection there is between correct ideas of the attributes of God, and the exercise of faith in him unto eternal life.

2. Let us here observe that the real design which the God of heaven had in view in making the human family acquainted with his attributes was that they, through the ideas of the existence of his attributes, might be enabled to exercise faith in him, and, through the exercise of faith in him, might obtain eternal life; for without the idea of the existence of the attributes which belong to God, the minds of men could not have power to exercise faith in him so as to lay hold upon eternal life. The God of heaven, understanding most perfectly the constitution of human nature and the weakness of men, knew what was necessary to be revealed, and what ideas must be planted in their minds in order that they might be enabled to exercise faith in him unto eternal life.

3. Having said so much, we shall proceed to examine the attributes of God, as set forth in his revelations to the human family and to show how necessary correct ideas of his attributes

are to enable men to exercise faith in him; for without these ideas being planted in the minds of men, it would be out of the power of any person or persons to exercise faith in God so as to obtain eternal life. So that the divine communications made to men in the first instance were designed to establish in their minds the ideas necessary to enable them to exercise faith in God, and through this means to be partakers of his glory.

4. We have, in the revelations which he has given to the human family, the following account of his attributes:

5. First—Knowledge. Acts 15:18: "Known unto God are all his works from the beginning of the world." Isaiah 46:9–10: "Remember the former things of old: for I am God, and there is none else; I am God, and there is none like me, *declaring the end from the beginning,* and from ancient times the things that are not yet done, saying, My counsel shall stand, and I will do all my pleasure," (italics added).

6. Secondly—Faith or power. Hebrews 11:3: "Through faith we understand that the worlds were framed by the word of God." Genesis 1:1: "In the beginning God created the heaven and the earth." Isaiah 14:24, 27: "The Lord of hosts hath sworn, saying, Surely as I have thought, so shall it come to pass; and as I have purposed, so shall it stand. . . . For the Lord of hosts hath purposed, and who shall disannul it? and his hand is stretched out, and who shall turn it back?"

7. Thirdly—Justice. Psalm 89:14: "Justice and judgment are the habitation of thy throne." Isaiah 45:21: "Tell ye, and bring them near; yea, let them take counsel together: who hath declared this from ancient time? . . . have not I the Lord? and there is no God else beside me; a just God and a Saviour." Zephaniah 3:5: "The just Lord is in the midst thereof." Zechariah 9:9: "Rejoice greatly, O daughter of Zion; shout, O daughter of Jerusalem: behold, thy King cometh unto thee: he is just, and having salvation."

8. Fourthly—Judgment. Psalm 89:14: "Justice and judgment are the habitation of thy throne." Deuteronomy 32:4: "He is the Rock, his work is perfect: for all his ways are judgment:

a God of truth and without iniquity, just and right is he." Psalm 9:7: "But the Lord shall endure for ever: he hath prepared his throne for judgment." Psalm 9:16: "The Lord is known by the judgment which he executeth."

9. Fifthly—Mercy. Psalm 89:14: "Mercy and truth shall go before thy face." Exodus 34:6: "And the Lord passed by before him, and proclaimed, The Lord, the Lord God, merciful and gracious." Nehemiah 9:17: "But thou art a God ready to pardon, gracious and merciful."

10. And sixthly—Truth. Psalm 89:14: "Mercy and truth shall go before thy face." Exodus 34:6: "Long-suffering; and abundant in goodness and truth." Deuteronomy 32:4: "He is the Rock, his work is perfect: for all his ways are judgment: a God of truth and without iniquity, just and right is he." Psalm 31:5: "Into thine hand I commit my spirit: thou hast redeemed me, O Lord God of truth."

11. By a little reflection, it will be seen that the idea of the existence of these attributes in the Deity is necessary to enable any rational being to exercise faith in him; for without the idea of the existence of these attributes in the Deity, men could not exercise faith in him for life and salvation; seeing that without the knowledge of all things God would not be able to save any portion of his creatures; for it is by reason of the knowledge which he has of all things, from the beginning to the end, that enables him to give that understanding to his creatures by which they are made partakers of eternal life; and if it were not for the idea existing in the minds of men that God had all knowledge, it would be impossible for them to exercise faith in him.

12. And it is not less necessary that men should have the idea of the existence of the attribute power in the Deity; for unless God had power over all things, and was able by his power to control all things, and thereby deliver his creatures who put their trust in him from the power of all beings that might seek their destruction, whether in heaven, on earth, or in hell, men could not be saved. But with the idea of the existence of this attribute planted in the mind, men feel as though they

had nothing to fear who put their trust in God, believing that he has power to save all who come to him to the very uttermost.

13. It is also necessary, in order to exercise faith in God unto life and salvation, that men should have the idea of the existence of the attribute justice in him; for without the idea of the existence of the attribute justice in the Deity, men could not have confidence sufficient to place themselves under his guidance and direction; for they would be filled with fear and doubt lest the judge of all the earth would not do right, and thus fear or doubt, existing in the mind, would preclude the possibility of the exercise of faith in him for life and salvation. But when the idea of the existence of the attribute justice in the Deity is fairly planted in the mind, it leaves no room for doubt to get into the heart, and the mind is enabled to cast itself upon the Almighty without fear and without doubt, and with the most unshaken confidence, believing that the judge of all the earth will do right.

14. It is also of equal importance that men should have the idea of the existence of the attribute judgment in God, in order that they may exercise faith in him for life and salvation; for without the idea of the existence of this attribute in the Deity, it would be impossible for men to exercise faith in him for life and salvation, seeing that it is through the exercise of this attribute that the faithful in Christ Jesus are delivered out of the hands of those who seek their destruction; for if God were not to come out in swift judgment against the workers of iniquity and the powers of darkness, his saints could not be saved; for it is by judgment that the Lord delivers his saints out of the hands of all their enemies, and those who reject the gospel of our Lord Jesus Christ. But no sooner is the idea of the existence of this attribute planted in the minds of men, than it gives power to the mind for the exercise of faith and confidence in God, and they are enabled by faith to lay hold on the promises which are set before them, and wade through all the tribulations and afflictions to which they are subjected by reason of the persecution from those who know not God, and obey not the gospel of our Lord Jesus

Christ, believing that in due time the Lord will come out in swift judgment against their enemies, and they shall be cut off from before him, and that in his own due time he will bear them off conquerors, and more than conquerors, in all things.

15. And again, it is equally important that men should have the idea of the existence of the attribute mercy in the Deity, in order to exercise faith in him for life and salvation; for without the idea of the existence of this attribute in the Deity, the spirits of the saints would faint in the midst of the tribulations, afflictions, and persecutions which they have to endure for righteousness' sake. But when the idea of the existence of this attribute is once established in the mind, it gives life and energy to the spirits of the saints, believing that the mercy of God will be poured out upon them in the midst of their afflictions, and that he will be compassionate to them in their sufferings, and that the mercy of God will lay hold of them and secure them in the arms of his love, so that they will receive a full reward for all their sufferings.

16. And lastly, but not less important to the exercise of faith in God, is the idea of the existence of the attribute truth in him; for without the idea of the existence of this attribute, the mind of man could have nothing upon which it could rest with certainty—all would be confusion and doubt. But with the idea of the existence of this attribute in the Deity in the mind, all the teachings, instructions, promises, and blessings become realities, and the mind is enabled to lay hold of them with certainty and confidence, believing that these things, and all that the Lord has said, shall be fulfilled in their time; and that all the cursings, denunciations, and judgments, pronounced upon the heads of the unrighteous, will also be executed in the due time of the Lord: and, by reason of the truth and veracity of him, the mind beholds its deliverance and salvation as being certain.

17. Let the mind once reflect sincerely and candidly upon the ideas of the existence of the before-mentioned attributes in the Deity, and it will be seen that, as far as his attributes are concerned, there is a sure foundation laid for the exercise of faith

in him for life and salvation. For inasmuch as God possesses the attribute knowledge, he can make all things known to his saints necessary for their salvation; and as he possesses the attribute power, he is able thereby to deliver them from the power of all enemies; and seeing, also, that justice is an attribute of the Deity, he will deal with them upon the principles of righteousness and equity, and a just reward will be granted unto them for all their afflictions and sufferings for the truth's sake. And as judgment is an attribute of the Deity also, his saints can have the most unshaken confidence that they will, in due time, obtain a perfect deliverance out of the hands of all their enemies, and a complete victory over all those who have sought their hurt and destruction. And as mercy is also an attribute of the Deity, his saints can have confidence that it will be exercised towards them, and through the exercise of that attribute towards them, comfort and consolation will be administered unto them abundantly, amid all their afflictions and tribulations. And, lastly, realizing that truth is an attribute of the Deity, the mind is led to rejoice amid all its trials and temptations, in hope of that glory which is to be brought at the revelation of Jesus Christ, and in view of that crown which is to be placed upon the heads of the saints in the day when the Lord shall distribute rewards unto them, and in prospect of that eternal weight of glory which the Lord has promised to bestow upon them, when he shall bring them in the midst of his throne to dwell in his presence eternally.

18. In view, then, of the existence of these attributes, the faith of the saints can become exceedingly strong, abounding in righteousness unto the praise and glory of God, and can exert its mighty influence in searching after wisdom and understanding, until it has obtained a knowledge of all things that pertain to life and salvation.

19. Such, then, is the foundation which is laid, through the revelation of the attributes of God, for the exercise of faith in him for life and salvation; and seeing that these are attributes of the Deity, they are unchangeable—being the same yesterday, to-day, and forever—which gives to the minds of the Latter-day

Saints the same power and authority to exercise faith in God which the Former-day Saints had; so that all the saints, in this respect, have been, are, and will be, alike until the end of time; for God never changes, therefore his attributes and character remain forever the same. And as it is through the revelation of these that a foundation is laid for the exercise of faith in God unto life and salvation, the foundation, therefore, for the exercise of faith was, is, and ever will be, the same; so that all men have had, and will have, an equal privilege.

QUESTIONS AND ANSWERS ON THE FOREGOING PRINCIPLES

20. What was shown in the third lecture?

It was shown that correct ideas of the character of God are necessary in order to exercise faith in him unto life and salvation; and that without correct ideas of his character, men could not have power to exercise faith in him unto life and salvation, but that correct ideas of his character, as far as his character was concerned in the exercise of faith in him, lay a sure foundation for the exercise of it (Lecture 4:1).

21. What object had the God of Heaven in revealing his attributes to men?

That through an acquaintance with his attributes they might be enabled to exercise faith in him so as to obtain eternal life (Lecture 4:2).

22. Could men exercise faith in God without an acquaintance with his attributes, so as to be enabled to lay hold of eternal life?

They could not (Lecture 4:2–3).

23. What account is given of the attributes of God in his revelations?

First, Knowledge; secondly, Faith or Power; thirdly, Justice; fourthly, Judgment; fifthly, Mercy; and sixthly, Truth (Lecture 4:4–10).

24. Where are the revelations to be found which give this relation of the attributes of God?

In the Old and New Testaments, and they are quoted in Lecture 4:5–10. [Let the student turn and commit these paragraphs to memory.]

25. Is the idea of the existence of these attributes in the Deity necessary in order to enable any rational being to exercise faith in him unto life and salvation?

It is.

26. How do you prove it?

By the eleventh, twelfth, thirteenth, fourteenth, fifteenth, and sixteenth paragraphs in this lecture. [Let the student turn and commit these paragraphs to memory.]

27. Does the idea of the existence of these attributes in the Deity, as far as his attributes are concerned, enable a rational being to exercise faith in him unto life and salvation?

It does.

28. How do you prove it?

By the seventeenth and eighteenth paragraphs. [Let the student turn and commit these paragraphs to memory.]

29. Have the Latter-day Saints as much authority given them, through the revelation of the attributes of God, to exercise faith in him as the Former-day Saints had?

They have.

30. How do you prove it?

By the nineteenth paragraph of this lecture. [Let the student turn and commit this paragraph to memory.]

LECTURE FIFTH

1. In our former lectures we treated of the being, character, perfections, and attributes of God. What we mean by perfections is, the perfections which belong to all the attributes of his nature. We shall, in this lecture, speak of the Godhead—we mean the Father, Son, and Holy Spirit.

2. There are two personages who constitute the great, matchless, governing, and supreme power over all things, by whom all things were created and made, that are created and made, whether visible or invisible, whether in heaven, on earth, or in the earth, under the earth, or throughout the immensity of space. They are the Father and the Son—the Father being a personage of spirit, glory, and power, possessing all perfection and fullness, the Son, who was in the bosom of the Father, a personage of tabernacle, made or fashioned like unto man, or being in the form and likeness of man, or rather man was formed after his likeness and in his image; he is also the express image and likeness of the personage of the Father, possessing all the fullness of the Father, or the same fullness with the Father; being begotten of him, and ordained from before the foundation of the world to be a propitiation for the sins of all those who should believe on his name, and is called the Son because of the flesh, and descended in suffering below that which man can suffer; or, in other words, suffered greater sufferings, and was exposed to more powerful contradictions than any man can be. But, notwithstanding all this, he kept the law of God, and remained without sin, showing thereby that it is in the power of man to keep the law and remain also without sin; and also, that

by him a righteous judgment might come upon all flesh, and that all who walk not in the law of God may justly be condemned by the law, and have no excuse for their sins. And he being the Only Begotten of the Father, full of grace and truth, and having overcome, received a fullness of the glory of the Father, possessing the same mind with the Father, which mind is the Holy Spirit, that bears record of the Father and the Son, and these three are one; or, in other words, these three constitute the great, matchless, governing and supreme power over all things; by whom all things were created and made that were created and made, and these three constitute the Godhead, and are one; the Father and the Son possessing the same mind, the same wisdom, glory, power, and fullness—filling all in all; the Son being filled with the fullness of the mind, glory, and power; or, in other words, the spirit, glory, and power, of the Father, possessing all knowledge and glory, and the same kingdom, sitting at the right hand of power, in the express image and likeness of the Father, mediator for man, being filled with the fullness of the mind of the Father; or, in other words, the Spirit of the Father, which Spirit is shed forth upon all who believe on his name and keep his commandments; and all those who keep his commandments shall grow up from grace to grace, and become heirs of the heavenly kingdom, and joint heirs with Jesus Christ; possessing the same mind, being transformed into the same image or likeness, even the express image of him who fills all in all; being filled with the fullness of his glory, and become one in him, even as the Father, Son, and Holy Spirit are one.

3. From the foregoing account of the Godhead, which is given in his revelations, the saints have a sure foundation laid for the exercise of faith unto life and salvation, through the atonement and mediation of Jesus Christ; by whose blood they have a forgiveness of sins, and also a sure reward laid up for them in heaven, even that of partaking of the fullness of the Father and the Son through the Spirit. As the Son partakes of the fullness of the Father through the Spirit, so the saints are, by the same Spirit, to be partakers of the same fullness, to enjoy the same

glory; for as the Father and the Son are one, so, in like manner, the saints are to be one in them. Through the love of the Father, the mediation of Jesus Christ, and the gift of the Holy Spirit, they are to be heirs of God, and joint heirs with Jesus Christ.

QUESTIONS AND ANSWERS ON THE FOREGOING PRINCIPLES

4. *Of what do the foregoing lectures treat?*
Of the being, perfections, and attributes of the Deity (Lecture 5:1).

5. *What are we to understand by the perfections of the Deity?*
The perfections which belong to his attributes.

6. *How many personages are there in the Godhead?*
Two: the Father and Son (Lecture 5:1).

7. *How do you prove that there are two personages in the Godhead?*
By the scriptures. Genesis 1:26 (JST Genesis 1:27; Moses 2:26); and Lecture 2:6: "And I, God, said unto mine Only Begotten, which was with me from the beginning, Let us make man in our image, after our likeness; and it was so." Genesis 3:22 (JST Genesis 3:28; Moses 4:28): "And I, the Lord God, said unto mine Only Begotten, Behold, the man is become as one of us, to know good and evil." John 17:5: "And now, O Father, glorify thou me with thine own self with the glory which I had with thee before the world was," (Lecture 5:2).

8. *What is the Father?*
He is a personage of glory and of power (Lecture 5:2).

9. *How do you prove that the Father is a personage of glory and of power?*
Isaiah 60:19: "The sun shall be no more thy light by day; neither for brightness shall the moon give light unto thee: but

the Lord shall be unto thee an everlasting light, and thy God thy glory." 1 Chronicles 29:11: "Thine, O Lord, is the greatness, and the power, and the glory." Psalm 29:3: "The voice of the Lord is upon the waters: the God of glory thundereth." Psalm 79:9: "Help us, O God of our salvation, for the glory of thy name." Romans 1:23: "And changed the glory of the uncorruptible God into an image made like to corruptible man." Secondly, of power. 1 Chronicles 29:11: "Thine, O Lord, is the greatness, and the power, and the glory." Jeremiah 32:17: "Ah Lord God! behold, thou hast made the heaven and the earth by thy great power and stretched out arm, and there is nothing too hard for thee." Deuteronomy 4:37: "And because he loved thy fathers, therefore he chose their seed after them, and brought thee out in his sight with his mighty power." 2 Samuel 22:33: "God is my strength and power." Job 26:7–14: "He stretcheth out the north over the empty place, and hangeth the earth upon nothing. He bindeth up the waters in his thick clouds; and the cloud is not rent under them. He holdeth back the face of his throne, and spreadeth his cloud upon it. He hath compassed the waters with bounds, until the day and night come to an end. The pillars of heaven tremble and are astonished at his reproof. He divideth the sea with his power, and by his understanding he smiteth through the proud. By his spirit he hath garnished the heavens; his hand hath formed the crooked serpent. Lo, these are parts of his ways: but how little a portion is heard of him? but the thunder of his power who can understand?"

10. What is the Son?

First, he is a personage of tabernacle (Lecture 5:2).

11. How do you prove it?

John 14:9–11: "Jesus saith unto him, Have I been so long time with you, and yet hast thou not known me, Philip? he that hath seen me hath seen the Father; and how sayest thou then, Shew us the Father? Believest thou not that I am in the

Father, and the Father in me? the words that I speak unto you I speak not of myself: but the Father that dwelleth in me, he doeth the works. Believe me that I am in the Father, and the Father in me." Secondly, and being a personage of tabernacle, was made or fashioned like unto man, or being in the form and likeness of man (Lecture 5:2). Philippians 2:5–8: "Let this mind be in you, which was also in Christ Jesus: who, being in the form of God, thought it not robbery to be equal with God: but made himself of no reputation, and took upon him the form of a servant, and was made in the likeness of men: and being found in fashion as a man, he humbled himself, and became obedient unto death, even the death of the cross." Hebrews 2:14, 16: "Forasmuch then as the children are partakers of flesh and blood, he also himself likewise took part of the same. . . . For verily he took not on him the nature of angels; but he took on him the seed of Abraham." Thirdly, he is also in the likeness of the personage of the Father (Lecture 5:2). Hebrews 1:1–3: "God, who at sundry times and in divers manners spake in time past unto the fathers by the prophets, hath in these last days spoken unto us by his Son, whom he hath appointed heir of all things, by whom also he made the worlds; who being the brightness of his glory, and the express image of his person." Again, Philippians 2:5–6: "Let this mind be in you, which was also in Christ Jesus: who, being in the form of God, thought it not robbery to be equal with God."

12. Was it by the Father and the Son that all things were created and made that were created and made?

It was. Colossians 1:15–17: "Who is the image of the invisible God, the firstborn of every creature: for by him were all things created, that are in heaven, and that are in earth, visible and invisible, whether they be thrones, or dominions, or principalities, or powers: all things were created by him, and for him: and he is before all things, and by him all things consist." Genesis 1:1: "In the beginning God created the heaven and the earth." Hebrews 1:2: "[God] hath in these last days spoken unto

us by his Son, whom he hath appointed heir of all things, by
whom also he made the worlds."

13. Does the Son possess the fullness of the Father?

He does. Colossians 1:19; 2:9: "For it pleased the Father
that in him should all fulness dwell." "For in him dwelleth all
the fulness of the Godhead bodily." Ephesians 1:23: "Which is
his [Christ's] body, the fulness of him that filleth all in all."

14. Why was he called the Son?

Because of the flesh. Luke 1:35: "That holy thing which
shall be born of thee, shall be called the Son of God." Matthew
3:16–17: "And Jesus, when he was baptized, went up
straightway out of the water, and, lo, the heavens were opened
unto him, and he [John] saw the Spirit of God descending like
a dove, and lighting upon him: and lo a voice from heaven,
saying, This is my beloved Son, in whom I am well pleased,"
(JST Matthew 3:45–46).

*15. Was he ordained of the Father, from before the foundation of
the world, to be a propitiation for the sins of all those who should
believe on his name?*

He was. 1 Peter 1:18–20: "Forasmuch as ye know that ye
were not redeemed with corruptible things, as silver and gold,
from your vain conversation received by tradition from your
fathers; but with the precious blood of Christ, as of a lamb
without blemish and without spot: who verily was foreordained
before the foundation of the world, but was manifest in these
last times for you." Revelation 13:8: "And all that dwell upon
the earth shall worship him [the beast], whose names are not
written in the book of life of the Lamb slain from the foundation of the world." 1 Corinthians 2:7: "But we speak the
wisdom of God in a mystery, even the hidden wisdom, which
God ordained before the world unto our glory."

16. Do the Father and the Son possess the same mind?

They do. John 5:30: "I [Christ] can of mine own self do nothing: as I hear, I judge: and my judgment is just; because I seek not mine own will, but the will of the Father which hath sent me." John 6:38: "For I [Christ] came down from heaven, not to do mine own will, but the will of him that sent me." John 10:30: "I [Christ] and my Father are one."

17. What is this mind?

The Holy Spirit. John 15:26: "But when the Comforter is come, whom I will send unto you from the Father, even the Spirit of truth, which proceedeth from the Father, he shall testify of me [Christ]." Galatians 4:6: "And because ye are sons, God hath sent forth the Spirit of his Son into your hearts."

18. Do the Father, Son, and Holy Spirit constitute the Godhead?

They do (Lecture 5:2). [Let the student turn and commit this paragraph to memory.]

19. Do the believers in Christ Jesus, through the gift of the Spirit, become one with the Father and the Son, as the Father and the Son are one?

They do. John 17:20–21: "Neither pray I for these [the apostles] alone, but for them also which shall believe on me through their word; that they all may be one; as thou, Father, art in me, and I in thee, that they also may be one in us: that the world may believe that thou hast sent me."

20. Does the foregoing account of the Godhead lay a sure foundation for the exercise of faith in him unto life and salvation?

It does.

21. How do you prove it?

By the third paragraph of this lecture. [Let the student turn and commit this paragraph to memory.]

LECTURE SIXTH

1. Having treated in the preceding lectures of the ideas, of the character, perfections, and attributes of God, we next proceed to treat of the knowledge which persons must have, that the course of life which they pursue is according to the will of God, in order that they may be enabled to exercise faith in him unto life and salvation.

2. This knowledge supplies an important place in revealed religion; for it was by reason of it that the ancients were enabled to endure as seeing him who is invisible. An actual knowledge to any person, that the course of life which he pursues is according to the will of God, is essentially necessary to enable him to have that confidence in God without which no person can obtain eternal life. It was this that enabled the ancient saints to endure all their afflictions and persecutions, and to take joyfully the spoiling of their goods, knowing (not believing merely) that they had a more enduring substance (Heb. 10:34).

3. Having the assurance that they were pursuing a course which was agreeable to the will of God, they were enabled to take, not only the spoiling of their goods, and the wasting of their substance, joyfully, but also to suffer death in its most horrid forms; knowing (not merely believing) that when this earthly house of their tabernacle was dissolved, they had a building of God, a house not made with hands, eternal in the heavens (2 Cor. 5:1).

4. Such was, and always will be, the situation of the saints of God, that unless they have an actual knowledge that the course they are pursuing is according to the will of God, they will grow

weary in their minds, and faint; for such has been, and always will be, the opposition in the hearts of unbelievers and those that know not God against the pure and unadulterated religion of heaven (the only thing which insures eternal life), that they will persecute to the uttermost all that worship God according to his revelations, receive the truth in the love of it, and submit themselves to be guided and directed by his will; and drive them to such extremities that nothing short of an actual knowledge of their being the favorites of heaven, and of their having embraced that order of things which God has established for the redemption of man, will enable them to exercise that confidence in him, necessary for them to overcome the world, and obtain that crown of glory which is laid up for them that fear God.

5. For a man to lay down his all, his character and reputation, his honor, and applause, his good name among men, his houses, his lands, his brothers and sisters, his wife and children, and even his own life also—counting all things but filth and dross for the excellency of the knowledge of Jesus Christ—requires more than mere belief or supposition that he is doing the will of God; but actual knowledge, realizing that, when these sufferings are ended, he will enter into eternal rest, and be a partaker of the glory of God.

6. For unless a person does know that he is walking according to the will of God, it would be offering an insult to the dignity of the Creator were he to say that he would be a partaker of his glory when he should be done with the things of this life. But when he has this knowledge, and most assuredly knows that he is doing the will of God, his confidence can be equally strong that he will be a partaker of the glory of God.

7. Let us here observe, that a religion that does not require the sacrifice of all things never has power sufficient to produce the faith necessary unto life and salvation; for, from the first existence of man, the faith necessary unto the enjoyment of life and salvation never could be obtained without the sacrifice of all earthly things. It was through this sacrifice, and this only,

that God has ordained that men should enjoy eternal life; and it is through the medium of the sacrifice of all earthly things that men do actually know that they are doing the things that are well pleasing in the sight of God. When a man has offered in sacrifice all that he has for the truth's sake, not even withholding his life, and believing before God that he has been called to make this sacrifice because he seeks to do his will, he does know, most assuredly, that God does and will accept his sacrifice and offering, and that he has not, nor will not seek his face in vain. Under these circumstances, then, he can obtain the faith necessary for him to lay hold on eternal life.

8. It is in vain for persons to fancy to themselves that they are heirs with those, or can be heirs with them, who have offered their all in sacrifice, and by this means obtained faith in God and favor with him so as to obtain eternal life, unless they, in like manner, offer unto him the same sacrifice, and through that offering obtain the knowledge that they are accepted of him.

9. It was in offering sacrifices that Abel, the first martyr, obtained knowledge that he was accepted of God. And from the days of righteous Abel to the present time, the knowledge that men have that they are accepted in the sight of God is obtained by offering sacrifice. And in the last days, before the Lord comes, he is to gather together his saints who have made a covenant with him by sacrifice. Psalms 50:3–5: "Our God shall come, and shall not keep silence: a fire shall devour before him, and it shall be very tempestuous round about him. He shall call to the heavens from above, and to the earth, that he may judge his people. Gather my saints together unto me; those that have made a covenant with me by sacrifice."

10. Those, then, who make the sacrifice, will have the testimony that their course is pleasing in the sight of God; and those who have this testimony will have faith to lay hold on eternal life, and will be enabled, through faith, to endure unto the end, and receive the crown that is laid up for them that love the appearing of our Lord Jesus Christ. But those who do not make the sacrifice cannot enjoy this faith, because men are

dependent upon this sacrifice in order to obtain this faith: therefore, they cannot lay hold upon eternal life, because the revelations of God do not guarantee unto them the authority so to do, and without this guarantee, faith could not exist.

11. All the saints of whom we have account, in all the revelations of God which are extant, obtained the knowledge which they had of their acceptance in his sight through the sacrifice which they offered unto him; and through the knowledge thus obtained their faith became sufficiently strong to lay hold upon the promise of eternal life, and to endure as seeing him who is invisible; and were enabled, through faith, to combat the powers of darkness, contend against the wiles of the adversary, overcome the world, and obtain the end of their faith, even the salvation of their souls.

12. But those who have not made this sacrifice to God do not know that the course which they pursue is well pleasing in his sight; for whatever may be their belief or their opinion, it is a matter of doubt and uncertainty in their mind; and where doubt and uncertainty are, there faith is not, nor can it be. For doubt and faith do not exist in the same person at the same time; so that persons whose minds are under doubts and fears cannot have unshaken confidence; and where unshaken confidence is not, there faith is weak; and where faith is weak, the persons will not be able to contend against all the opposition, tribulations, and afflictions which they will have to encounter in order to be heirs of God, and joint heirs with Christ Jesus; and they will grow weary in their minds, and the adversary will have power over them and destroy them.

[This lecture is so plain, and the facts set forth so self-evident that it is deemed unnecessary to form a catechism upon it; the student is, therefore, instructed to commit the whole to memory.]

Lecture Seventh

1. In the preceding lessons, we treated of what faith was, and of the object on which it rested. Agreeable to our plan, we now proceed to speak of its effects.

2. As we have seen in our former lectures that faith was the principle of action and of power in all intelligent beings, both in heaven and on earth, it will not be expected that we shall, in a lecture of this description, attempt to unfold all its effects; neither is it necessary to our purpose so to do, for it would embrace all things in heaven and on earth, and encompass all the creations of God, with all their endless varieties; for no world has yet been framed that was not framed by faith, neither has there been an intelligent being on any of God's creations who did not get there by reason of faith as it existed in himself or in some other being; nor has there been a change or a revolution in any of the creations of God, but it has been effected by faith; neither will there be a change or a revolution, unless it is effected in the same way, in any of the vast creations of the Almighty, for it is by faith that the Deity works.

3. Let us here offer some explanation in relation to faith, that our meaning may be clearly comprehended. We ask, then, what are we to understand by a man's working by faith? We answer—we understand that when a man works by faith, he works by mental exertion instead of physical force. It is by words, instead of exerting his physical powers, with which every being works when he works by faith. God said, "Let there be light: and there was light." Joshua spake, and the great lights which God had created stood still. Elijah commanded, and the

heavens were stayed for the space of three years and six months, so that it did not rain: he again commanded and the heavens gave forth rain. All this was done by faith. And the Saviour says, "If you have faith as a grain of mustard seed, say to this mountain, 'Remove,' and it will remove; or say to that sycamine tree, 'Be ye plucked up, and planted in the midst of the sea,' and it shall obey you," (Genesis 1:3; Joshua 10:12–13; 1 Kings 17:1; 18:1, 41–45; Matthew 17:20; Luke 17:6). Faith, then, works by words; and with these its mightiest works have been, and will be, performed.

4. It surely will not be required of us to prove that this is the principle upon which all eternity has acted and will act; for every reflecting mind must know that it is by reason of this power that all the hosts of heaven perform their works of wonder, majesty, and glory. Angels move from place to place by virtue of this power; it is by reason of it that they are enabled to descend from heaven to earth; and were it not for the power of faith they never could be ministering spirits to them who should be heirs of salvation, neither could they act as heavenly messengers, for they would be destitute of the power necessary to enable them to do the will of God.

5. It is only necessary for us to say that the whole visible creation, as it now exists, is the effect of faith. It was faith by which it was framed, and it is by the power of faith that it continues in its organized form, and by which the planets move round their orbits and sparkle forth their glory. So, then, faith is truly the first principle in the science of Theology, and, when understood, leads the mind back to the beginning, and carries it forward to the end; or, in other words, from eternity to eternity.

6. As faith, then, is the principle by which the heavenly hosts perform their works, and by which they enjoy all their felicity, we might expect to find it set forth in a revelation from God as the principle upon which his creatures here below must act in order to obtain the felicities enjoyed by the saints in the eternal world; and that, when God would undertake to raise up men for the enjoyment of himself, he would teach them the

necessity of living by faith, and the impossibility there was of their enjoying the blessedness of eternity without it, seeing that all the blessings of eternity are the effects of faith.

7. Therefore it is said, and appropriately too, that "Without faith it is impossible to please God," (Hebrews 11:6). If it should be asked—Why is it impossible to please God without faith? The answer would be—Because without faith it is impossible for men to be saved; and as God desires the salvation of men, he must, of course, desire that they should have faith; and he could not be pleased unless they had, or else he could be pleased with their destruction.

8. From this we learn that the many exhortations which have been given by inspired men, to those who had received the word of the Lord to have faith in him, were not mere commonplace matters, but were for the best of all reasons, and that was—because without it there was no salvation, neither in this world nor in that which is to come. When men begin to live by faith they begin to draw near to God; and when faith is perfected, they are like him; and because he is saved, they are saved also; for they will be in the same situation he is in, because they have come to him; and when he appears they shall be like him, for they will see him as he is.

9. As all the visible creation is an effect of faith, so is salvation also—we mean salvation in its most extensive latitude of interpretation, whether it is temporal or spiritual. In order to have this subject clearly set before the mind, let us ask what situation must a person be in, in order to be saved? Or what is the difference between a saved man and one who is not saved? We answer: from what we have before seen of the heavenly worlds, they must be persons who can work by faith and who are able, by faith, to be ministering spirits to them who shall be heirs of salvation; and they must have faith to enable them to act in the presence of the Lord, otherwise they cannot be saved. And what constitutes the real difference between a saved person and one not saved is—the difference in the degree of their faith—one's faith has become perfect enough to lay hold upon eternal life,

and the other's has not. But to be a little more particular, let us ask—Where shall we find a prototype into whose likeness we may be assimilated, in order that we may be made partakers of life and salvation? Or, in other words, where shall we find a saved being? For if we can find a saved being, we may ascertain without much difficulty what all others must be in order to be saved. We think that it will not be a matter of dispute, that two beings who are unlike each other cannot both be saved; for whatever constitutes the salvation of one will constitute the salvation of every creature which will be saved; and if we find one saved being in all existence, we may see what all others must be, or else not be saved. We ask, then, where is the prototype? Or, where is the saved being? We conclude, as to the answer of this question, there will be no dispute among those who believe the Bible, that it is Christ: all will agree in this, that he is the prototype or standard of salvation; or, in other words, that he is a saved being. And if we should continue our interrogation, and ask how it is that he is saved? The answer would be—because he is a just and holy being; and if he were anything different from what he is, he would not be saved; for his salvation depends on his being precisely what he is and nothing else; for if it were possible for him to change, in the least degree, so sure he would fail of salvation and lose all his dominion, power, authority, and glory, which constitute salvation; for salvation consists in the glory, authority, majesty, power, and dominion which Jehovah possesses and in nothing else; and no being can possess it but himself or one like him. Thus says John, in his first epistle, third chapter, second and third verses: "Beloved, now are we the sons of God, and it doth not yet appear what we shall be; but we know that, when he shall appear, we shall be like him, for we shall see him as he is. And every man that hath this hope in him purifieth himself, even as he is pure." Why purify themselves as he is pure? Because if they do not they cannot be like him.

10. The Lord said unto Moses, (Leviticus 19:2): "Speak unto all the congregation of the children of Israel, and say unto them, Ye shall be holy: for I the Lord your God am holy." And

Peter says in his first epistle, verses 15–16: "But as he which hath called you is holy, so be ye holy in all manner of conversation; because it is written, Be ye holy; for I am holy." And the Saviour says, (Matthew 5:48): "Be ye therefore perfect, even as your Father which is in heaven is perfect." If any should ask, why all these sayings? The answer is to be found from what is before quoted from John's epistle, that when he (the Lord) shall appear, the saints will be like him; and if they are not holy, as he is holy, and perfect, as he is perfect, they cannot be like him; for no being can enjoy his glory without possessing his perfections and holiness, no more than they could reign in his kingdom without his power.

11. This clearly sets forth the propriety of the Saviour's saying, recorded in John's testimony, 14:12: "Verily, verily, I say unto you, He that believeth on me, the works that I do shall he do also; and greater works than these shall he do; because I go unto my Father." This taken in connection with some of the sayings in the Saviour's prayer, recorded in the seventeenth chapter, gives great clearness to his expressions. He says in the twentieth to twenty-fourth verses (John 17:20–24): "Neither pray I for these alone, but for them also which shall believe on me through their word; that they all may be one; as thou, Father, art in me, and I in thee, that they also may be one in us: that the world may believe that thou hast sent me. And the glory which thou gavest me I have given them; that they may be one, even as we are one: I in them, and thou in me, that they may be made perfect in one; and that the world may know that thou hast sent me, and hast loved them, as thou hast loved me. Father, I will that they also, whom thou hast given me, be with me where I am; that they may behold my glory, which thou hast given me: for thou lovedst me before the foundation of the world."

12. All these sayings put together give as clear an account of the state of the glorified saints as language could give—the works that Jesus had done they were to do, and greater works than those which he had done among them should they do, and

that because he went to the Father. He does not say that they should do these works in time; but they should do greater works, because he went to the Father. He says in the twenty-fourth verse: "Father, I will that they also, whom thou hast given me, be with me where I am; that they may behold my glory." These sayings, taken in connection, make it very plain that the greater works which those that believed on his name were to do were to be done in eternity, where he was going and where they should behold his glory. He had said, in another part of his prayer, that he desired of his Father that those who believed on him should be one in him, as he and the Father were one in each other. "Neither pray I for these [the apostles] alone, but for them also which shall believe on me through their word; that they all may be one"; that is, they who believe on him through the apostles' words, as well as the apostles themselves, "that they all may be one; as thou, Father, art in me and I in thee, that they also may be one in us," (John 17:20–21).

13. What language can be plainer than this? The Saviour surely intended to be understood by his disciples, and he so spake that they might understand him; for he declares to his Father, in language not to be easily mistaken, that he wanted his disciples, even all of them, to be as himself and the Father, for as he and the Father were one so they might be one with them. And what is said in the twenty-second verse is calculated to more firmly establish this belief, if it needs anything to establish it. He says: "And the glory which thou gavest me I have given them; that they may be one, even as we are one." As much as to say that unless they have the glory which the Father had given him, they could not be one with them; for he says he had given them the glory that the Father had given him that they might be one; or, in other words, to make them one.

14. This fills up the measure of information on this subject, and shows most clearly that the Saviour wished his disciples to understand that they were to be partakers with him in all things, not even his glory excepted.

15. It is scarcely necessary here to observe what we have previously noticed, that the glory which the Father and the Son have is because they are just and holy beings; and that if they were lacking in one attribute or perfection which they have, the glory which they have never could be enjoyed by them, for it requires them to be precisely what they are in order to enjoy it; and if the Saviour gives this glory to any others, he must do it in the very way set forth in his prayer to his Father—by making them one with him as he and the Father are one. In so doing, he would give them the glory which the Father has given him; and when his disciples are made one with the Father and Son, as the Father and the Son are one, who cannot see the propriety of the Saviour's saying—"The works that I do shall he do also; and greater works than these shall he do; because I go unto my Father," (John 14:12).

16. These teachings of the Saviour most clearly show unto us the nature of salvation, and what he proposed unto the human family when he proposed to save them—that he proposed to make them like unto himself, and he was like the Father, the great prototype of all saved beings; and for any portion of the human family to be assimilated into their likeness is to be saved; and to be unlike them is to be destroyed; and on this hinge turns the door of salvation.

17. Who cannot see, then, that salvation is the effect of faith? For, as we have previously observed, all the heavenly beings work by this principle; and it is because they are able so to do that they are saved, for nothing but this could save them. And this is the lesson which the God of heaven, by the mouth of all his holy prophets, has been endeavoring to teach to the world. Hence we are told, that "Without faith it is impossible to please God," (Hebrews 11:6); and that salvation "is of faith, that it might be by grace; to the end the promise might be sure to all the seed," (Romans 4:16). And that Israel, who followed after the law of righteousness, has not attained to the law of righteousness. "Wherefore? Because they sought it not by faith, but as it were by the works of the law. For they stumbled at that

stumblingstone," (Romans 9:32). And Jesus said unto the man who brought his son to him, to get the devil who tormented him cast out: "If thou canst believe, all things are possible to him that believeth," (Mark 9:23). These with a multitude of other scriptures which might be quoted plainly set forth the light in which the Saviour, as well as the Former-day Saints, viewed the plan of salvation. That it was a system of faith—it begins with faith, and continues by faith; and every blessing which is obtained in relation to it is the effect of faith, whether it pertains to this life or that which is to come. To this, all the revelations of God bear witness. If there were children of promise, they were the effects of faith, not even the Saviour of the world excepted. "Blessed is she that believed," said Elizabeth to Mary, when she went to visit her, "for there shall be a performance of those things which were told her from the Lord," (Luke 1:45). Nor was the birth of John the Baptist the less a matter of faith; for in order that his father Zacharias might believe, he was struck dumb. And through the whole history of the scheme of life and salvation, it is a matter of faith: every man received according to his faith—according as his faith was, so were his blessings and privileges; and nothing was withheld from him when his faith was sufficient to receive it. He could stop the mouths of lions, quench the violence of fire, escape the edge of the sword, wax valiant in fight, and put to flight the armies of the aliens; women could, by their faith, receive their dead children to life again; in a word, there was nothing impossible with them who had faith. All things were in subjection to the Former-day Saints, according as their faith was. By their faith they could obtain heavenly visions, the ministering of angels, have knowledge of the spirits of just men made perfect, of the general assembly and church of the firstborn, whose names are written in heaven, of God the judge of all, of Jesus the Mediator of the new covenant, and become familiar with the third heavens, see and hear things which were not only unutterable, but were unlawful to utter (Hebrews 11–12). Peter, in view of the power of faith, says to the Former-day Saints

(2 Peter 1:2–3): "Grace and peace be multiplied unto you, through the knowledge of God, and of Jesus our Lord, according as his divine power hath given unto us all things that pertain unto life and godliness, through the knowledge of him that hath called us to glory and virtue." In the first epistle (of Peter), first chapter, third to fifth verses, he says: "Blessed be the God and Father of our Lord Jesus Christ, which according to his abundant mercy hath begotten us again unto a lively hope by the resurrection of Jesus Christ from the dead, to an inheritance incorruptible and undefiled, and that fadeth not away, reserved in heaven for you, who are kept by the power of God through faith unto salvation ready to be revealed in the last time."

18. These sayings put together show the apostle's views most clearly, so as to admit of no mistake on the mind of any individual. He says that all things that pertain to life and godliness were given unto them through the knowledge of God and our Saviour Jesus Christ. And if the question is asked, how were they to obtain the knowledge of God? (For there is a great difference between believing in God and knowing him—knowledge implies more than faith. And notice, that all things that pertain to life and godliness were given through the knowledge of God) the answer is given—through faith they were to obtain this knowledge; and, having power by faith to obtain the knowledge of God, they could with it obtain all other things which pertain to life and godliness.

19. By these sayings of the apostle, we learn that it was by obtaining a knowledge of God that men got the knowledge of all things which pertain to life and godliness, and this knowledge was the effect of faith, so that all things which pertain to life and godliness are the effects of faith.

20. From this we may extend as far as any circumstances may require, whether on earth or in heaven, and we will find it the testimony of all inspired men, or heavenly messengers, that all things that pertain to life and godliness are the effects of faith and nothing else; all learning, wisdom, and prudence fail,

and everything else as a means of salvation but faith. This is the reason that the fishermen of Galilee could teach the world—because they sought by faith, and by faith obtained. And this is the reason that Paul counted all things but filth and dross—what he formerly called his gain he called his loss; yea, and he counted all things but loss for the excellency of the knowledge of Christ Jesus the Lord (Philippians 3:7–10). Because to obtain the faith by which he could enjoy the knowledge of Christ Jesus the Lord, he had to suffer the loss of all things. This is the reason that the Former-day Saints knew more, and understood more, of heaven and of heavenly things than all others beside, because this information is the effect of faith—to be obtained by no other means. And this is the reason that men, as soon as they lose their faith, run into strifes, contentions, darkness, and difficulties; for the knowledge which tends to life disappears with faith, but returns when faith returns; for when faith comes, it brings its train of attendants with it—apostles, prophets, evangelists, pastors, teachers, gifts, wisdom, knowledge, miracles, healings, tongues, interpretation of tongues, etc. All these appear when faith appears on earth, and disappear when it disappears from the earth; for these are the effects of faith, and always have attended, and always will, attend it. For where faith is, there will the knowledge of God be also, with all things which pertain thereto—revelations, visions, and dreams, as well as every necessary thing, in order that the possessors of faith may be perfected, and obtain salvation; for God must change, otherwise faith will prevail with him. And he who possesses it will, through it, obtain all necessary knowledge and wisdom, until he shall know God, and the Lord Jesus Christ, whom he has sent—whom to know is eternal life. Amen.

INDEX

References are to lecture and paragraph numbers.
Lecture numbers are in bold type.

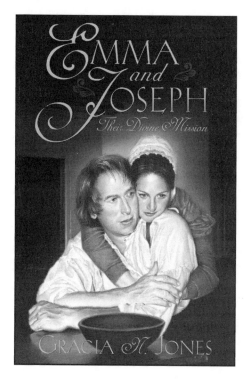

The Patriarchal Office

The little apartment above the Whitney store in Kirtland was the scene of many profound events, including the School of the Prophets, meetings of the brethren, sacred visions and revelations, and ordinances. The purpose and the organization of the Church were being defined. It became clear that the Church was to be directed under the same order as was outlined by Paul in the New Testament, with apostles, prophets, evangelists, deacons, teachers, and priests. Joseph Smith, Sr., was called to be the evangelist, or presiding patriarch, to the Church.[46] On 18 December 1833, Joseph blessed his father and set him apart to this office. He and his counselors, Sidney Rigdon and Frederick G. Williams, laid their hands on Father Smith's head and ordained him. Oliver Cowdery wrote the blessings as they were given.

A year after this ordination, on 9 December 1834, Father Smith, acting in his office as Church Patriarch, gave blessings to Joseph and Emma.

Patriarchal Blessings

Patriarchal blessings are most sacred and personal to the one receiving them. The Prophet Joseph, as head of the dispensation of the fullness of times, and Emma, as his wife, hold a particularly personal relationship to every soul who embraces the gospel. Because of this, these precious documents do not belong only to their direct descendants; they belong to all.

Joseph's patriarchal blessing gives a glimpse into the place he holds in the eternal scheme of things, as head of the last dispensation. It also sheds some light upon what was being hinted at in the 1830 revelation to Emma, when she was told to rejoice in the "glory" that was to come upon her husband. Although it may seem that Emma is consigned to a reflected glory, the position she holds as wife of the Prophet Joseph Smith is glorious and encompasses great responsibility, both for herself and for her posterity. Both of these blessings define the glorious responsibility of the Prophet and his wife and, especially in the case of Joseph's blessing, transcend mortal expectations. In it we find out a great deal about the biblical Joseph, who was sold into Egypt; we better understand the hopes this Joseph had for the future, knowing that in the latter-days, he would have a name-sake who would fulfill a divine mission. Whereas Joseph of old provided grain to save a starving Israel, the latter-day prophet, Joseph would provide sustenance for the soul. Through him the gathering of latter-day Israel would be accomplished, whether from mortal toil or by his sustaining effort from beyond the veil.

The inclusion of these blessings here provides one of the rare occasions for us to read words spoken personally by Joseph Sr.

Joseph's Patriarchal Blessing

Joseph Smith, My son, I lay my hands upon thy head in the name of the Lord Jesus Christ, to confirm upon thee a father's blessing. The Lord thy God has called thee by name out of the heavens. Thou hast heard his voice from on high, from time to time, even in thy youth. The hand of the angel of his presence has been extended toward thee, by which thou hast been lifted up and sustained; yea, the Lord has delivered thee from the hands of thine enemies; and thou hast been made to rejoice in his salvation: thou hast sought to know his ways, and from thy childhood thou hast meditated much upon the great things of his law. Thou hast suffered much in thy youth, and the poverty and afflictions of thy father's family have been a grief to thy soul. Thou hast desired to see them delivered from bondage, for thou hast loved them with a perfect love. Thou hast stood by thy Father, and . . . would have covered his nakedness rather than see him exposed to shame; when the daughters of the gentiles laughed, thy heart has been moved with a just anger to avenge thy kindred. Thou hast been an obedient son and the commands of thy Father, and the reproofs of thy mother, thou has respected and obeyed—for all of these things the Lord my God will bless thee. Thou hast been called, even in thy youth to the great work of the Lord, to do a work in this generation which no other man would do as thyself, in all things according to the will of the Lord. A marvelous work and a wonder has the Lord wrought by thy hand, even that which shall prepare the way for the remnants of his people to come in among the gentiles, with their fullness, as the tribes of Israel are restored. I bless thee with the blessings of thy forefathers, Abraham, Isaac, and Jacob; . . .

CONTINUED IN

EMMA *and* JOSEPH
Their Divine Mission